ATHENA
RISING

ATHENA
RISING

How and Why
Men Should
Mentor Women

W. BRAD JOHNSON, PhD,
and DAVID SMITH, PhD

First published by Bibliomotion, Inc.
39 Harvard Street
Brookline, MA 02445
Tel: 617-934-2427
www.bibliomotion.com

Printed in the United States of America

Library of Congress Cataloging-in-Publication Data

Names: Johnson, W. Brad, author. | Smith, David (David Glenn), 1965- author.
Title: Athena rising : how and why men should mentor women / W. Brad Johnson,
    PhD, and David Smith, PhD.
Description: Brookline, MA : Bibliomotion, Inc., [2016] | Includes
    bibliographical references and index.
Identifiers: LCCN 2016024746| ISBN 9781629561516 (hardcover : alk. paper) |
    ISBN 9781629561530 (enhanced ebook)
Subjects: LCSH: Mentoring in business. | Mentoring in the professions. |
    Women employees. | Women executives. | Women in the professions. | Sex
    role in the work environment.|
Classification: LCC HF5385 .J637 2016 | DDC 658.3/124082—dc23
LC record available at https://lccn.loc.gov/2016024746

*With deepest gratitude and admiration, this book is dedicated to
two remarkable women:*
Brad's sister, Navy Captain Shannon Jill Johnson
David's daughter, Julia Caroline Smith

And to a generation of fiercely courageous rising Athenas:
*Every woman who has graduated from one of America's service academies
since the first class of resolute women shattered barriers
and led the way for their sisters at Annapolis, West Point, and
Colorado Springs in the fall of 1976.*

CONTENTS

FOREWORD

By Betsy Myers

Brad Johnson and David Smith have struck upon something incredibly significant in the field of leadership and the advancement of women—*the importance of engaging men to mentor women.*

Why does this matter?

Well, let's start with the staggering 2016 statistics. Women currently hold just 10 to 15 percent of the senior leadership (C-Suite) positions in corporate America and the majority of organizations. And in the military, women make up just 16.6 percent of the officer corps and 7.1 percent of the top ranks of generals and admirals.

This is startling, given that women now represent 58 percent of our college graduates and hold 50 percent of middle-management positions—with 40 percent holding positions that include purchasing authority.

Yes, of course, there has been progress; and yes, today we have more female leaders than a generation ago. But only a very small portion is sitting *at the top of organizations.*

It's not for lack of trying, or from a lack of good intentions. No, the unfortunate truth is that what has historically passed for gender efforts inside corporate America has often just been a series of discussions, classes, and conferences in which women find themselves talking to women.

The backdrop here, as we all know, is that talent is a key motivator in today's competitive global marketplace and CEOs and savvy business leaders understand that they must have a workforce that reflects the current and future workplace and customer. They also know that the female perspective often leads to wiser decisions, and the rich relationship skills that women leaders offer frequently result in happier employees and deeper client connections.

The good news is that the vast majority of corporate CEOs no longer ask "why" they should include and advance women in their organizations. But what still eludes us is the "how"—how to include, keep, and advance women in organizations.

Research shows us that men mentoring women can make all the difference to their retention and advancement.

A 2014 gender parity study by Bain & Company, for example, found that nearly half of women enter the workforce with their eye on the C-Suite, but their confidence and ambition levels drop 60 percent after more than just two years on the job. One of the key insights was that marital and parental status did not really differ between women who aspire and those who do not. Instead, women lack meaningful recognition, support, and mentorship from their managers, which is necessary to shape and support their path to advancement.

Brad and Dave give us a brilliant—but simple—strategy that combines mentorship of women with the trusted collaboration of men.

Because men remain the most powerful stakeholder group in most organizations, I strongly believe that this powerful combination will allow us to accelerate our gender progress. I also believe that this book will become an invaluable tool for any organization looking to increase its success with precious female talent.

Betsy Myers is a leadership expert, author, and advocate, who is also speaking at and convening workshops around the world on the changing nature of leadership and women's leadership. Her book, *Take the Lead: Motivate, Inspire, and Bring Out the Best in Yourself and Everyone Around You,* was released in September 2011. Her experience spans the corporate, political, and higher education arena. She is the founding director of the Center for Women and Business at Bentley University and served as the executive director of the Center for Public Leadership at Harvard's Kennedy School of Government. Myers was a senior adviser to two U.S. presidents, the COO and chair of Women for

President Obama's 2008 national presidential campaign, and during the Clinton Administration, she launched, and was the first director of, the White House Office for Women's Initiatives and Outreach. She also served as the director of the Office of Women's Business Ownership at the SBA. Prior to joining the Clinton Administration, Myers spent six years building Myers Insurance and Financial Services in Los Angeles specializing in the small business and women's market. She received her Bachelor's degree in Business Administration from the University of San Diego and her Master's degree in Public Administration from Harvard's Kennedy School, where she was also a public service fellow.

PREFACE

This is a guide for men.

We are writing this book for our genetic brothers, men who are upright, courageous, and visionary in their sense of how a just and dignified workplace should look—for men *and* women. This is a guy's guide to leveling the playing field for women through the medium of intentional and powerful mentorships. For too long, most of us have been part of the problem. Rewarded from birth merely for owning a penis, we're all silent beneficiaries—or whistling bystanders—in a world that persists in keeping women on the sidelines, excluded from key leadership roles, and earning less pay for equal work.

Gentlemen, this is a call to arms. In education, business, the military, and organizations of all stripes, we are in a battle for talent. Organizations and professions that exclude or marginalize 50 percent of the workforce—including half of those at the top of the curve on intellectual, emotional, and creative giftedness—are doomed. Those companies and institutions that deliberately include women in key leadership positions are simply more effective, balanced, and geared for long-term success. These are organizations that benefit from the distinctive and powerful gifts that each gender contributes to innovation and execution. Workplaces defined by flexibility, collaboration, and caring are much more likely to exist when women are deliberately integrated and valued at all levels of leadership. Welcoming and promoting women is simply key to long-term organizational survival.

Yet women today remain under-recruited, under-compensated, and certainly, under-promoted to the upper echelons of power and leadership. And when they do get in the door, they face deliberate exclusion or an insidious—and possibly more painful—disregard fueled by stereotypes, hypercompetitive masculine work settings, and, sometimes, out-and-out hostility toward women in the workplace.

Think we're exaggerating? As we sit down to begin writing this book in the summer of 2015, a Nobel Prize–winning British scientist has just proclaimed that "girls" should never be allowed to work in research labs with men. Why? Well, because, "you fall in love with them, they fall in love with you, and when you criticize them they cry. . . ."[1] And a recent news article about women staffers on Capitol Hill reveals that they are often barred from ever being alone or—God forbid—ever being seen after hours with their male bosses for fear of rumors and bad publicity for the male legislators.[2] And the coup de grâce, our own Marine Corps recently fired a female recruit commander for being "too aggressive and abrasive."[3] Seriously, can you imagine a male Marine being called "too aggressive and abrasive"? Let's face it, guys, we are only scratching the surface here; you see examples of women being minimized, marginalized, cut out, and derided, merely for their gender, nearly anywhere you look. The problem, of course, is that we—men, dudes, guys, fellas, bros . . . *gentlemen*—rarely say much about it. And far too few of us actually *do* anything about it. Yet, we ignore this state of affairs to the detriment of our organizations; our own daughters, wives, and other women we care about; and even our own personal success and quality of life.

Strong mentoring relationships alter lives, not merely careers. Four decades of research on mentoring leaves no room for doubt about the impact of mentoring on career success and the ability to thrive in adult life. The benefits to the mentee can be so valuable that identification with at least one important mentor should be considered a major developmental task of the early career years. As ardent consumers of the latest mentoring research, you can trust us on this one, gentlemen: the effects of strong mentoring are remarkable, profound, and enduring; mentoring relationships have the capacity to transform individuals, groups, organizations, and communities.

And while we're on the topic of benefits, what's in it for you? The data is pretty clear. Mentors reap profound satisfaction from "giving" to the next generation and guiding talented junior members of the profession, male and female. If you've ever mentored someone, then you also appreciate how mentoring leads to new insights, key insider information about the organization, and a larger network of colleagues over time. You will learn as much about yourself from your mentee as she will learn from you. The interpersonal skills you hone through mentorship will serve you well as you rise through the ranks.

But here is the rub: although mentorship appears even more crucial for women when it comes to career advancement, women often have a tougher time securing mentors. And when they do, they often reap fewer career and psychosocial benefits than men. As the goddess Athena discovered in pursuing her own adventures as a woman in a male-dominated world: gender matters!

About now, you might be asking: Why can't women mentor women? There are several reasons. In many male-centric domains, senior women may be nowhere in sight or when they are visible may be reluctant to mentor other women. And the truth is that men are still more likely to hold senior leadership positions in most professions, businesses, and organizations—face it, in many cases there just aren't enough senior women around.

So why don't we (guys) mentor women often and easily? Men are too often reticent to engage promising women in the workplace, for lots of reasons. Some of us just aren't sure how to have a professional relationship with a woman. Some of us worry she'll think we're coming on to her (and sometimes we worry we might indeed be coming on). At other times, we may be anxious about gossip and innuendo around the office. (e.g., *I'll look creepy. They'll think we're dating or something. What if someone tells my girlfriend/wife?*). We'd be lying if we didn't admit that many of us have at one time worried that we might slip and say or do the wrong thing leading to a sexual harassment case—yikes, who needs that! And finally, let's not forget that most of us continue to harbor implicit biases about women (e.g., *They can't take the demands of the job. They're not as capable as men. She should be at home*).

Men, it is time. If you are reading this guide, then you *know* it is time. It is time to fully accept the critical role we can play in pulling women up and pushing them forward. Just as Sheryl Sandberg has recently called women to "lean in" to their careers, we are calling men to lean in to the task of mentoring women. We are not asking you to mentor women exclusively or to ignore talented junior men—far from it. We are merely asking that you open your eyes, recognize some of the talented women down the hall, in the boardroom, or in the classroom, and then widen your circle of mentees to include them! Chances are, every man brave enough to be reading this page can play a crucial role—*this year*—in helping several promising junior women to persist, advance, and thrive in their profession or workplace. So gentlemen, time to lock and load! As men in positions of influence, we have all got to be more effective at mentoring rising stars of both genders—particularly in the multitude of environments where senior women are few.

This is a *practical* guide for men. It is a manual for mentoring women consciously and deliberately. Part 1 of this guide provides the background intel you'll need to better understand women, yourself as a man, and the varieties of male–female relationships. Part 2 details the nuts and bolts or the *key elements* of being an effective mentor for women. In the pages of part 2, we'll show you how women often need mentoring with a different character, a unique style, and, sometimes, a focus beyond just career. Each chapter in part 2 contains several distinct elements, key strategies for becoming more effective in your mentoring relationships with women. Together, these chapters constitute our "Manual for Men" on how to effectively engage, encourage, promote, and sponsor talented women at work. Excellent mentoring is equal parts art and science. It demands self-awareness, emotional intelligence, relationship know-how, political savvy, and, of course, a genuine desire to see a good person thrive in her career.

Each element, or mentoring function, covered in part 2 blends crucial knowledge, attitudes, and skills. Some of the elements emphasize specific career-promotion strategies while others focus on the mentee's personal growth and well-being. Think of each element as a critical tool in the toolbox of a master carpenter. The skillful carpenter understands that he cannot use all his tools at once and that not every tool will be required for each job. Experience, discernment, and discretion are required.[4]

Finally, let's talk about the elephant in the room. We are two guys writing a book about mentoring women. Weird? Yes and no. We are good friends, naval officers (one former, one current), college professors (a psychologist and a sociologist), and men who have long been concerned about the struggle of women to earn a place at the leadership table—particularly in the military, but in other typically male settings as well. Yet, we are humble outsiders to the female experience. No amount of concern for the plight of our female colleagues can make us experts on the experience of *being* a woman in the workplace. So, early on in our planning and brainstorming for this guide, we did two things. First, we distilled the latest evidence about effective mentorship, cross-gender relationships at work, and what women say is most helpful to them in mentorships. Second, we reached out to a substantial number of high-flying, successful women in a wide array of professions and organizations, and we asked them about their own experiences with male mentors. We wanted to hear their stories and learn about what worked well for them in relationships with senior men. We asked about how the relationships got started and precisely what these men did that was most helpful in the relationship.

Following, we include the list of women who helped us with our quest to better understand male–female mentorships. We think you will agree they constitute an all-star cast. We are deeply grateful for their stories and reflections and we include some of their most salient experiences in part 2 to illustrate the "how to" of being an excellent mentor for women. If there are any errors, oversights, or bloopers in the pages that follow, they are undoubtedly the work of your authors.

Gentlemen, thank you for taking this mission seriously. Thank you for opening your heart and mind to those everyday Athenas—talented young women who only need a fair chance and an equal start. By mentoring women intentionally and conscientiously, you'll change women's lives, improve the work environment, and make your organization more competitive. And, in the end, you'll be a better man.

Brad Johnson and David Smith
August 2015

Rohini Anand, PhD, Sodexo Senior Vice President and Global Chief Diversity Officer

Laura Behling, PhD, Dean and Vice President for Academic Affairs, Knox College

Dana Born, PhD, Air Force Brigadier General (ret), Currently: Lecturer at Harvard University

Virginia Brodie, Marine Corps Second Lieutenant, first female Combat Artillery Officer

Susan Chambers, Walmart Executive Vice President, Global People Division

Alice Eagly, PhD, Professor of Psychology at Northwestern University, Gender Expert

Deborah Gillis, President and CEO, Catalyst

Rebecca Halstead, Army Brigadier General (ret), Founder Steadfast Leadership

Kathy Hannan, Partner for Diversity and Corporate Responsibility, KPMG

Katie Higgins, Marine Corps Captain, first female Blue Angels pilot

Michelle Howard, Four-Star Navy Admiral, Vice Chief of Naval Operations

Nadine Kaslow, PhD, Emory University Professor, 2014 President of the American Psychological Association

Susan Madsen, EdD, Utah Valley University, Utah Women & Leadership Project

Betsy Myers, Adviser to Presidents Clinton and Obama, Currently: Founding Director of the Center for Women & Business at Bentley University

Camille Nichols, Army Major General, Commanding General Contracting Command

Janet Petro, Deputy Director, John F. Kennedy Space Center

Sheryl Sandberg, Facebook Chief Operating Officer and Founder of LeanIn.Org

Sandra Stosz, Coast Guard Rear Admiral, Currently: USCG Academy Superintendent

Tabitha Strobel, Navy Lieutenant, first woman to serve on a submarine crew

Kathy Waller, CFO and Executive Vice President, Coca-Cola Company

PART I

Background Intel

1

The Everyday Athena

July 1, 2004, United States Naval Academy, Annapolis, Maryland;
Plebe Summer, Day 2

It's 5:30 in the morning. Suddenly, a metal pipe clangs down the concrete corridor in Bancroft Hall, shattering silence and wrenching Katie from a few short hours of sleep. Her eyes fly open and she sits bolt upright in unfamiliar surroundings, heart pounding like a jackhammer. Two seconds later someone—actually, it sounds like several someones—is pounding on the door and screaming orders full blast. Something about, "Get up, get dressed, and fall in, now!" Her roommates of less than twenty-four hours explode from their bunks, equally terrified and disoriented. The three of them fumble desperately for their physical training gear, pulling on shorts, T-shirts, and running shoes. A quick glance in the mirror shows Katie's newly cut chin-length hair; she feels like Bozo the Clown. She pointlessly tries to tame it with a splash of water. Fearful of being late, the three roommates race into the too-bright corridor to stand at attention with thirty equally shell-shocked eighteen-year-olds. It is still dark outside.

Fifteen minutes later, Katie has joined 1,188 other plebes for a long session of push-ups, sit-ups, pull-ups, and all varieties of calisthenics, followed by a long run along the Severn River. As the sun comes up she wonders if she was crazy to devote so much effort to earning top grades, top SAT scores, a congressional nomination, and, eventually, a coveted appointment to the U.S. Naval Academy. As she looks around, she sees that less than a quarter of the new plebe class is female. For the first time, she feels like a minority. Although she thought she was in peak physical shape as a high school varsity athlete, her legs feel like rubber from the "six round trips," and she wonders if she'll be able to keep up with the guys. As she runs in formation with her company, she is sweating profusely in the already humid air. Later, she knows she'll be at the firing range, tackling the obstacle course, learning to march, practicing standard sailing and seamanship commands, and beginning a series of demanding summer courses. In between each of these events, she takes advantage of every minute to memorize the seemingly never-ending list of daily minutiae, traditions, customs, and history that her upperclassmen demand she regurgitate without error and with confidence and conviction. Failure to do so would bring unwanted attention.

How often had her high school friends told her she was crazy to do this? For the first time Katie wonders if they were right. She wonders if she'll make it to graduation and commissioning four long years down the road. She's always been tough, always self-assured, and always up for a challenge, but this seems like something else altogether. As one of the company upperclassmen jogs next to her barking orders and critiquing her form, she hopes she'll find the support she needs to make it through the Naval Academy gauntlet.

July 2014, United States Naval Air Station, Pensacola, Florida

U.S. Marine Corps Captain Katie Higgins is designated as a pilot for the famous Navy Flight Demonstration Squadron, the Blue Angels. Having logged more than four hundred combat hours as a Marine Corps pilot, she is the first woman to be designated a Blue Angel since the inception of the elite team in 1946.

We count ourselves fortunate. We get to work with rising stars like Katie every day. Each morning, we drive through the gates of our nation's premier educational institution for Navy and Marine Corps officers to find academy midshipmen up early exercising, participating in military drills, and preparing for a full day of demanding engineering-oriented classes, athletic practice, and leadership training. Why do they prepare so diligently? After all, they're just college kids! The answer is both sobering and awe-inspiring. In just four short years, those who make it through the academy will be commissioned as officers; each of them must be prepared to immediately lead Sailors and Marines in combat, and lead them well.

Katie and the other remarkable young women at the U.S. Naval Academy—academically and athletically gifted women who have decided to tackle a rigorous program historically open only to men—prepare for careers as combat leaders despite all forces working against them.

We refer to these young women as *everyday Athenas*. You may recall that in Greek mythology, Athena was the goddess of the arts, reason, wisdom, and war. As the patron goddess of heroic endeavor, she was often a shrewd companion of heroes. Although Athena is typically depicted holding a spear and wearing a golden helmet—as though preparing to attack—she is known in mythology not only for her status as fierce warrior, but also for her role as diplomat, mediator, and wise advisor. Though she is the goddess of war strategy, she preferred to resolve conflicts through wisdom and reason whenever possible. As some Athena scholars have observed: "Wise, courageous, humane, and cooperative, Athena represents the best of all of us."[1]

We think the goddess Athena perfectly captures the character, wisdom, courage, and promise of female midshipmen at the Naval Academy. We choose to regard each of them as rising stars who have taken the more difficult path through life and career—women in a military culture dominated by men.

This chapter will briefly address the importance of *perception*. If men decide to frame the women they encounter at work as talented, capable, likely to succeed, and unique in terms of the gifts and skills linked to the feminine gender, then the obligation and inclination to help them as mentors will be glaring and unavoidable. See her as a rising Athena, not just a girl. Promise dwells in the eye of the beholder. We think that everyday Athenas at the Naval Academy serve as a nice exemplar for how to "see" women more generally. Finally, we will show how even future highfliers, women like Captain Katie Higgins, may need help to bridge the leadership-ambition gap identified by Sheryl Sandberg. Men must double down on deliberately helping female mentees to broaden their perspectives on what they can do and what they can achieve as leaders in their careers.

PERCEIVING EVERYDAY ATHENAS

Whether at the boardroom table or the break room table, women are more likely to be overlooked or just plain ignored by men. Sometimes, they don't even get a seat at the table. And when they do get a seat, their ideas and contributions are not always taken seriously. Thinking about her own early career experience at the executive table, Kathy Hannan, partner for diversity and corporate responsibility for KPMG, said, "I had been sitting around the key leadership table. At times, I would make a comment and it would get a tepid response, maybe some head nodding. Then, two or three people down the line, a male says exactly what I just said and everyone says 'wow' and starts discussing it like it's a new idea." Several women interviewed for this book recounted stories in which their input was dismissed by male bosses; some felt so undervalued that they quit contributing their insights.

In the twenty-first-century workplace, how do we make sense of these women's experiences? When asked, men often fail to even recognize that these dismissive episodes are occurring. Our tendency as men is to unknowingly sell women at work short, largely as a by-product of the way we have come to understand men's and women's roles in society. Despite the fact that there are almost twice as many women in the workforce today, by percentage, than there were in 1950, we still find persistent stereotypes about women's roles at work and home. Automatic perceptions and assumptions that women are nurturing, warm, and communal may sound positive, yet they can be limiting and undermine women's opportunities to compete and excel in the workplace. Our gendered perceptions make it too easy to overlook those everyday Athenas around us.

As you can surmise, our biased man perceptions about women create for them a prickly *double bind*. On one hand, we may perceive our female mentees as compassionate and caring nurturers but in so doing we may be unable to envision them as the "take charge and move out" leaders we need for key projects and challenging missions. In a similar vein, men may avoid recommending women for assignments that are too challenging or "in the trenches" because we don't see them as capable or aspiring to these tasks. Sometimes, our deeply engrained protective *man script*s get triggered. When this happens, our efforts to "protect" a talented woman actually sabotage her opportunity to compete and prove herself. In our world, the U.S. military, these stereotypes reinforce the perception that women are better suited for staff or support roles than for operational "combatant" roles that lead to the higher echelons of power and leadership.

Unfortunately, the negative consequences of our man perceptions don't end there. For instance, women who are directive and authoritative at work often get labeled "dragon ladies" and "iron bitches"; they are perceived to be coldhearted, abrasive, and bossy. As guys, we tend to steer clear of these women, often some of the most promising future leaders for our organizations and our nation. And if we find strong women noxious in some way, what does that say about our ability to see them as potential mentees? What are the chances we'll seek them out, engage, and begin providing crucial career support? In part 2 of this guide, "Mentoring Women: A Manual for Men," we'll challenge you to not reinforce these unrealistic perceptions when women at work demonstrate confident, decisive, and industrious behavior.

Volumes of social psychology research reveal that men evaluate certain behaviors quite differently when exhibited by a man or a woman. If you think you judge John's behavior the same as Jill's—even in identical situations—you're kidding yourself. For instance, as guys we might be comfortable with yelling at work, or give each other a pass when it happens—what dude doesn't lose his temper on occasion? But what about a woman who yells? Well, she's got to be overemotional or dangerous—return of the "PMSing dragon lady." And if a woman cries, well...what's new? But for a dude to cry or tear up when getting critical feedback...now, that's awkward, just plain "unmanly." Our perceptions about "appropriate" emotions create another double bind for women. If *she* doesn't cry she's cold and emotionless. But if *he* is dry eyed we applaud him for controlling his emotions. Getting the picture? Women who aspire to rise through the ranks and assume leadership roles must confront persistent double binds and inconsistent standards for leadership potential.

Just as important for women at work is what men fail to perceive. The perception that women are nurturing and caring is largely based on our experience of seeing women in family roles as primary caregivers. In fact, women in general *do* perform more childcare and household chores than men. Evidence shows that working women are 60 percent more likely than men to have full-time working spouses.[2] Why is this important? Because dual-career families have more challenges related to childcare and managing a household, and women in these families end up doing the lion's share of the domestic work. And, of course, mothers are seen as less committed to their careers. This affects wages, promotions, and hiring, a de facto "motherhood penalty."[3] Effective male mentors must become alert to stereotypical perceptions of women in the workplace and then find strategies for mitigating their effects on the promising women they champion.

FRAMING ENCOUNTERS AT WORK

Angela had finally landed a major account and just finished the final touches on her proposal presentation to the partners for the next day. Now she was considering what to wear. She wanted to present an image of confidence and competence—dressed to kill—yet maintain her personal sense of self as both competitive *and* feminine. Ultimately, she decided on a dark "power suit" with pants, white open-neck blouse with a gold necklace, heels, hair down, and a little less makeup than she would normally wear in a social setting.

The next day, during the presentation, all seemed to be going well. At the table were the senior partners, all men, who were nodding with approval as she delivered the presentation. What Angela didn't see was that some of the men were distracted by her attractiveness. In fact, one of them was brazenly staring at her cleavage. When she finished, the group was uncharacteristically quiet. There were no questions. Although Angela missed her effect on the men in the room, her mentor, Charles, did not. He made a mental note to have an honest conversation with the senior partner about the way the men in the room reacted to Angela. The leering and the silent treatment—Charles suspected this had more to do with inattention than disapproval of Angela's work—were flat-out inappropriate, unprofessional, and had to stop. Later he would also follow-up with Angela to make her aware of how her attractiveness would likely influence men's perceptions of her generally, and how her awareness of this fact would be important for her success moving forward.

Everyone wants to make a good impression at work. Effective impression management begins with identifying a desired social impression and then managing our own behavior to achieve the preferred effect. But often, women face more obstacles to coming across as competent, professional, and credible. One of those obstacles, highlighted in Angela's story, is the perception that women must choose between attractiveness and competence. Too often, everyday Athenas are subject to visual inspection, leers, and flirtatious comments from men that serve to undermine their sense of selves as rising professionals. A good mentor won't hesitate to address these reactions openly with the offending men, while helping the mentee develop strategies for neutralizing unwanted sexual attention and redirecting the focus to her competence, performance, and success.

Beyond the more obvious visual cues and attraction-based perceptions, women may also struggle when it comes to taking explicit credit for their contributions and achievements. This may be particularly challenging in team environments where it is not clear who is responsible for the team's successes.[4] In these contexts, men will naturally speak up for themselves and take credit. Taking credit may not come as naturally for even the best and brightest women. Proactive mentors explicitly encourage women to communicate their successes and accomplishments, and are their behind-the-scenes champions in settings where they can't necessarily advocate for themselves.

A final factor that can sharply define the way a woman is perceived at work is her apparent access to power in the organization. Because men and women network differently, women are sometimes seen as less connected to power sources than their male counterparts, resulting in fewer assignments to high-profile projects and fewer opportunities for advancement up the corporate ladder.

Women's professional networks tend to include primarily other women. But because there are more men in the power-holding positions in most organizations, women are less often networked with men who could effectively promote them for key opportunities and jobs. The lack of connection with men—potential sponsors and career champions—in their networks, coupled with their lower status at work, often creates more disadvantages for the everyday Athena.[5]

Ironically, unequal access to resources is particularly evident for women in more cohesive and project-based teams.[6] In the military, we build cohesion and group identity during training that result in loyalty and commitment—strong relational ties—to both the team and the mission. Researchers have discovered that information flow in cohesive teams is more likely to be within the same gender, making critical information gender exclusive.[7] Closed networks limit information flow to those with the strongest ties and exclude outsiders and those with weaker ties—women.[8] Because more gender-diverse networks rely on inclusivity and open information flow, they are more beneficial to women.[9] Effective male allies for women not only are loyal and proactive sponsors, they are furthermore proactive in shaping diverse network architectures for women. Teams with diverse networks reduce disadvantage for women and increase retention and promotion of our best and brightest.

Athena is rising. Women are entering the workplace in increasing numbers—including more than half of management positions—yet organizations continue to experience poor retention and promotion of the talented women they spend so much to recruit and train. As men concerned about the future of our organizations and the glaring gender gap in the C-suite, we must work to create effective networks and constellations of support for the women we champion.

BRIDGING THE CAREER-AMBITION GAP

Throughout our interviews with the highly accomplished women who shared their stories with us, two common experiences on the road to success occurred over and over again: first was the difficult journey these women faced to achieving mastery of the most important skill sets in their career fields and second was the presence of influential people who recognized their accomplishments and championed their cause. In fact, these two factors are considered essential for career ambition in *both* women and men.[10]

With some exceptions, the playing field in the workplace is leveling out. Women increasingly have opportunities to master essential career skills and compete at the highest levels. So why do we still find fewer women promoted to the higher levels of leadership? The stress and pressure associated with significant leadership roles can dissuade *both* men and women from seeking advancement.[11] And both men and women worry that they will be unable to balance work and family commitments as they progress up the corporate ladder. But here is the truth: men remain more likely to advance and stay on track with their careers than women.[12]

While the satisfaction of a job well done is sometimes enough to keep us motivated on the arduous journey to the top, for most of us, long-term career persistence requires more than self-motivation. Early in our careers, when we feel like imposters, we need affirmation that we belong. We also need encouragement, support, and the message from someone we admire that he or she believes that we have what it takes. Those champions of our lives and careers, the ones who recognize our potential and then affirm it out loud over and over again, are our mentors.

As men, we have learned to seek recognition for our accomplishments. Women, on the other hand, have learned that talking about their achievements is not culturally feminine. Instead, they divert attention and credit to someone else or even to luck. It requires an astute and persistent mentor to affirm and promote women's accomplishments so that their career aspirations and ambitions are fueled and endorsed.

At all levels of management and leadership, women report lower aspirations than men to advance to the higher levels of the organization. Women more than men find that the workplace disadvantages them based on gender. McKinsey & Company's 2015 report *Women in the Workplace* finds that even at the entry level almost 25 percent of women have experienced some gender obstacle at work that they feel has detracted from a raise, promotion, or assignment.[13] Chances are, the women you work with are feeling something similar.

Gentlemen, it's time to get busy. There's a lot we need to learn about women and the way the presence and persistence of women in organizations add to both the bottom line and the quality of life for both genders. Deliberately and skillfully mentoring women is an opportunity for us to open our minds, listen, and become better employees, colleagues, and men. We should approach everyday Athenas with authentic respect, openness, and encouragement, and in a spirit of collaboration. Healthy and productive mentoring relationships with women will require equal parts commitment and humility.

The past few decades have proven that trying to "fix" women to make them more like men in the workplace is not a viable pursuit, nor does it yield a desired outcome. For women and men to succeed at work, we need to take a page out of the military strategist's book and look for an asymmetric solution—to change the way we fight, or in this case, the way we work. We see evidence that this is occurring in a variety of occupations and professions as senior leaders begin to acknowledge the contributions and talents women bring to their businesses. Even the most traditional of male professions, the military, is instituting gender equality across all military occupational specialties and increasing parental leave, on-site childcare availability, career path flexibility, and dual-career family-friendly policies.[14] As thoughtful, dedicated, and forward-leaning men, we are responsible for first seeing, then valuing, and ultimately advocating for everyday Athenas around us.

2

How Women Struggle at Work

Let Us Count the Ways

Although women hear the mantra "Find a mentor if you want to make it" even before they show up for their first day of work, the plain truth is that women face far more hurdles than men when it comes to securing mentors, and even when they do, they are more likely to be disappointed with the quality of mentoring they receive. As we shall see in this chapter, girls are *still* not allowed in many "boys only" clubhouses. But now the stakes are much higher. Women face many varieties of bias and stereotype, and they are more likely to be discredited as leaders. Not only do powerful gender stereotypes exist, but women begin to accept and internalize the stereotypes. For our female colleagues, and potential mentees, this can translate into self-doubt and even shame. We should not, therefore, be surprised that women are more vulnerable to distress and loneliness at work. And when it comes to mentoring, they are too often forced to choose between unavailable, distant women and men who frankly just don't get it.

Let us be perfectly honest, gentlemen: men have had it pretty darn good. In our postindustrial society, work outside the home has been the inarguable domain of men. For decades, our masculine identity has been synonymous with the frequency of promotions and the size of our paychecks. While our outside employment has been honored and prioritized, women have been relegated to the domestic sphere as primary caregivers for the family. If women pursued their own careers, well, that was fine, as long as it didn't interfere with their "women's work" at home.

My, how things are changing! Gender roles in society—including the workplace—are shifting all around us. Thanks to the evolution of technology and automation, brute strength is no longer a job requirement in most fields. And women are having fewer children; thanks to medical technology, they can decide if and when they have children. In the last century, more women entered the workforce, often for reasons of necessity, to help the family make ends meet. Today, women launch careers for most of the same reasons that drive men. Yet, despite changing gender norms and the influx of women in the workforce, we still don't see many women in senior management and key leadership positions. And even when women make it to the C-suite and the corner office, substantial wage gaps serve to remind them that, well, they're just not men. What's going on?

FIGHT CLUB FOR GUYS, SOCIAL SKILLS FOR GIRLS

Compared to the women around us, we men are more likely to have been socialized to compete. In sports, in school, and most definitely on the playground, boys endure a time-honored finishing school, the curriculum of which includes independence, stoic toughness, and above all, competition for a spot in the pecking order. During our formative teenage years, when our gender identity is in constant need of reinforcement, we learn to compete in everything; our masculinity is at risk if we don't measure up—think double-dog dare![1] Of course, this background leaves us ideally suited for male-dominated work environments. We find it perfectly reasonable, even tantalizing, when a company or institution fosters a boot camp mentality and emphasizes culling the herd.

Just as boys learn to become competitive, girls often learn to avoid competition. Girls are more likely to behave according to societal gender roles when in proximity to boys. In fact, research comparing girls at coeducational and single-sex high schools showed that lower competitiveness occurred only at coeducational schools.[2] If girls are socialized to be less competitive, they may be more likely to opt out of competitive work environments. Women who enter traditionally masculine occupations often find it challenging to work in a competitive environment designed by and for men. And in these competitive landscapes, women achieve fewer promotions and pay raises.

Unlike guys, women are more often socialized to prioritize cooperation, interactive learning, sharing, and the harmonizing of work and personal life. This is precisely why research shows that women who attend all-women's colleges emerge far more confident and self-assured than those who attend predominantly male schools (e.g., science, engineering, business). Women immersed in chiding, competition, and sometimes out-and-out rejection by masculine "weed-out" systems take a serious hit to their self-confidence. As men who aspire to push women forward, we have first got to take a serious look at the forces that undermine and stifle women at work.

NO GIRLS ALLOWED!

Most guys reading this book are homosocials. You heard us right. When we engage in homosocial behavior we give preference to members of our own gender. Men do this by inviting only men—their bros at work, junior versions of themselves—into the guild. Look at those you currently mentor. Are they largely male? Would a woman have a tough time gaining entry to your network of knowledge, influence, and key connections? If the answer is yes, and if there are women in need of mentoring at your place of employment, then you might be a practicing homosocial.

Too often, women are unintentionally or, worse, deliberately excluded from crucial social engagement with men at work. Men tend to form workplace networks that provide access to information and resources leading to success at work, whereas women's networks are more likely to be based on providing emotional support and personal relationships. As guys, we often combine work relationships with social relationships outside the workplace. In many instances, these social extensions of our workplace connections occur on the golf course or over drinks at the local bar, contexts not conducive to the inclusion of women colleagues who may have family obligations or have to contend with coworkers' perceptions. Be honest, have you ever not invited a woman to a social event just because you thought she wouldn't be interested? When a woman does finally appear in a male-dominated field, she may be viewed as unnatural or too masculine, and subsequently ridiculed, rejected, and marginalized. In asserting herself at work, her highly competent and capable behavior is perceived by others as socially deficient and unlikable. Sadly, women may naturally attribute this social isolation and exclusion from the "the boy's club" to their own shortcomings. The backlash effects they feel at work for acting counterstereotypically can have long-term economic and social effects. For instance, in one creative study of junior university faculty, new professors were asked to keep a diary checklist of their developmental (mentoring) interactions with high-status colleagues (senior professors, deans). At the end of the semester, men had on average thirteen more interactions with power brokers. Score another one for the guys.

BARRIERS AND BIASES FOR WOMEN AT WORK

Hundreds of research studies leave little doubt. Compared with men, women face a host of biased assumptions and stereotyped thoughts about their basic competence, let alone their credibility as rising stars and future leaders. As a modern man, you may consider yourself immune to these backward and outdated attitudes. You might ask why we are asking you to revisit and reflect on gender biases. Answer: even guys who "get it" when it comes to women at work still harbor biases; we are human, after all. Decades of research on implicit bias show that many of us have been exposed to stereotypes about women throughout our lives. We're not talking exclusively about bias *against* women—gender bias can also come in the form of a preference *for* men. This exposure is so pervasive and saturating that gender bias often occurs automatically and unconsciously. To be effective mentors for women we must acknowledge and become more aware of these unconscious biases.

Here are some of the most pervasive and pernicious attitudes about women at work.[3] Read them with openness and honesty, gentlemen. If you do, it will be difficult not to feel empathy for women trying to break through in your profession.

Prove It Again

Women often have to prove themselves over and over in order to be seen as equally competent to men, especially in leadership positions. Stereotypical beliefs about women call into question their abilities when occupying high-status leadership positions. Even when women signal high competence in the form of educational attainment and work accomplishments, they can still be penalized by their male bosses because they pose a threat to the gender hierarchy.[4]

Women's performance evaluations can be tricky. Bias and stereotypes play an interesting role in evaluating performance and measuring competence. If a woman isn't perceived as nice, if she doesn't lead in a stereotypical feminine (collaborative, participative) way, she may receive more negative evaluations. Imagine the challenge she faces when she's got to get tough, mete out discipline, or deliver negative feedback to a man! Because stereotypes inform us that women won't be competent in leadership roles, their work performance is scrutinized more than men's. Objective criteria for success are often applied strictly to women while men . . . well, not so much. Guys often get a free pass based on our "potential" rather than our actual performance. When women achieve success it is often attributed to luck instead of competence, whereas the opposite is true for men. And assessing team performance also disadvantages women. Research studies reveal that when there is ambiguity as to who contributed to the team's success, women are judged less competent, less influential, and less likely to have a leadership role in the team.[5]

Of course, as guys, we may ask why women don't speak up and set the record straight. Here is the answer: women are socialized to be collaborative and relational and are likely to avoid focusing on their individual contributions in favor of supporting the team. While self-promotion for men is acceptable in the competitive work environment, women learn to avoid it. Too many times, they've witnessed the backlash when a woman openly takes credit for her hard work. How dare she try to be assertive!

Similarly, women are less likely than men to raise their hand for that job opportunity if they feel like they are not qualified or lack experience.

Much as women show aversion to competition, they are also more likely to avoid risk—especially at work.[6] Men have been socialized to take risks (it's a challenge) and believe that although they may not have the experience or qualifications, they'll learn along the way.

The Tightrope

Women often find themselves in a painful double-bind dilemma about how to behave at work. Behave like a woman and they face the prove-it-again bias and trigger stereotypes about being too "nice," "soft," or "timid" to make it. Behave like a man and they're "bitches" or "ballbusters" with poor social skills, leading to rejection from the guy's club. You see the bind. Feminine women aren't taken seriously. Masculine women are labeled too prickly to work with and kicked to the curb.

The gendered nature of work and division of household labor continue to reinforce these gender stereotypes in the workplace. The tension between nice/feminine and assertive/competitive can leave women off balance and anxious. While men find the competitive workplace natural, even invigorating, women are walking the tightrope, struggling with perceptions and figuring out how they should behave in the next interaction. If their gendered behavior at work feels inauthentic, the incongruence between their "real" and "ideal" selves may not only affect their work performance but also spill over into their family life.

The Maternal Wall

One of the most difficult barriers for women to contend with at work is the assumption that they are only marginally committed to their careers and that they will inevitably leave their jobs—no matter their position or tenure—and, God forbid, bear children. Even single women with no plans to have children may be seen implicitly as baby machines, ticking time bombs of maternity with all the demands and distractions associated with motherhood. The underlying assumption here is that women—by default—will always be primary caregivers, regardless of their unique family status or their partner's employment status. Although recent trends in the workforce provide a more nuanced story (e.g., women make up 40 percent of sole and primary breadwinners for families with children;[7] fathers are spending three times as many hours performing childcare and twice as much time doing housework as they did in 1965[8]), mothers are still doing more childcare and housework, even as they are increasing their work hours.

Should women decide to lean in and enjoy both career and motherhood, men may secretly or openly malign them for neglecting their maternal duties. Even if men don't openly say or suggest that women are neglecting their maternal duties, societal expectations of the *good mother* often create tension for career-oriented women that can leave them struggling with doubt, even shame. When women do decide to pause or exit their jobs to attend fully to parenthood, interviews suggest their decision often has more to do with inflexible and unsatisfying work environments than it does with the allure of full-time mothering.

Double Jeopardy

As if things weren't challenging enough for women at work, there is evidence that women of color must contend with *both* gender *and* racial bias. One African American aphorism captures the experience of women of color at work: "You have to work twice as hard to get half as far."[9] Compared with men or women generally, women of color are more likely to experience workplace interactions described as demeaning, disrespectful, and isolating. Evidence also indicates that women of color are more likely than any other group to experience workplace harassment.[10] As with any bias or prejudice in the workplace, people who don't feel valued, respected, or a sense of belonging have higher turnover intentions and job burnout and lower job satisfaction.[11]

Women As Leaders? What...?

Social psychologists long ago demonstrated that most of us—male and female—tend to see women in favorable terms; that is, understanding, kind, nurturing, and helpful. This is the often-replicated "women-are-wonderful effect." Sounds like a good thing for women, right? Not when it comes to leadership. Most of us—again, male and female—tend to define good leaders as action oriented, ambitious, dominant, competitive, self-sufficient, and willing to impose (his) will on others, for the most part, traits we associate with men. If women are wonderful and men take action the way leaders should, then many women with terrific leadership potential will be caught in a bind: be warm, friendly, and "nice" (feminine) or take charge, kick ass, and behave the way we expect leaders to act—and risk the negative backlash that often afflicts "masculine" women.

Not a rosy picture? Well, there are some best practices from women who have succeeded in the workplace. Alice Eagly and Linda Carli recommend women adopt the label of *tempered radicals* as "people who want to succeed in their organizations yet want to live by their values or identities, even if they are somehow at odds with the dominant culture of their organizations."[12] Some tempered radical strategies for women include: (1) striking a balance between a natural communal style and an agentic masculine style that will be understood by men at work; in other words, a woman must firmly direct others while being supportive, and (2) establishing her competence in key management roles by performing beyond expectations and ensuring she is recognized. Recognition should come through collaborative relationships and colleagues rather than self-promotion. Finally, building social capital through networks of men and women in positions of power and influence will help her gain recognition and establish a productive career.

Stereotype Threat

Often, a woman can be undermined merely by being reminded that she is a woman right before a crucial assessment or performance. Consider this study conducted by Claude Steele and his team of researchers at Stanford University. In one condition, men and women were told they were about to complete a test of mathematical ability that would then be used to compare men and women in the experiment. In this condition, women scored significantly lower than men on the test. In the second condition, a different group of men and women was simply informed that they would be working on a problem-solving exercise with no mention of a test, mathematics, or ability. There was no suggestion that men's and women's scores would be compared. In this condition (same exact math test administered), women's scores were far higher and not significantly different than the average for men in this condition.[13] See what's going on here? When you remind a person of a stereotype shortly before she must perform (e.g., women aren't good at math or science, women aren't as good at men at taking exams), focusing on the stereotype often lowers performance. Steele called this *stereotype threat,* and it is pervasive for women at work.[14] Each time men roll their eyes, snicker, and shake their heads as a woman tries to take on a traditionally masculine task, we are guilty of throwing up a barrier for women that we ourselves rarely face.

Although stereotype threat is pervasive in the workplace, men can help improve the work environment for women. In later studies, colleagues of Steele found that a workplace free from stereotype threat could be created if women are reminded that key tasks are not affected by or related to gender.[15] Other studies show that women who are exposed to role models that counter stereotypes often exhibit higher levels of performance. This is the phenomenon of *stereotype reactance.*[16] Visible, engaging, and successful senior women make a difference in the aspirations and self-confidence of young women in the workplace.

Stress and Loneliness

Because women are socialized to value and define themselves in terms of relationships, they are more often affected by the relational losses associated with entering or leaving college, employment, and even role shifts within a company or organization. Particularly when she is a gender minority at work, a woman may experience a greater hit to her self-esteem and social well-being when she has to change jobs and say goodbye to supportive colleagues—even when the reason for leaving is a well-deserved promotion. Moreover, studies show that because women bear the lion's share of caring for children, elderly parents, and even spouses outside of work, they are simply more vulnerable to periodic stress, anxiety, and exhaustion. And let's not forget the stressors and developmental concerns unique to women who defer entering the workforce until midlife in order to raise children. Excellent mentors recognize, appreciate, and demonstrate empathy for these extra burdens women face at work.

CAN'T WOMEN MENTOR WOMEN? NOT SO MUCH

It is tempting for men to assume that women can just get the mentoring they need from other women. Not so fast. In many academic departments, law firms, businesses, and professions, women are few and far between—especially women holding rank and power. While we see the number of women in early and mid-career management positions increasing at a high rate, the proportion of women at senior levels of management in the corporate C-suites has increased at a much lower rate—there are just fewer senior women available to mentor rising Athenas. When women are a clear minority, they sometimes avoid mentoring junior women, owing to competition for the few positions open to women or out of concern for the extra visibility and scrutiny that may accompany same-gender sponsorship, especially if the mentee does not perform well. Some have termed this reluctance to intervene on behalf of junior women a *silent betrayal*. And former U.S. Secretary of State Madeleine Albright famously remarked: "There is a special place in hell for women who don't help other women!"

But let's be fair. There are plenty of other good reasons why women can't get mentored by more senior women. If they achieve promotion and climb the ladder, senior women may be overburdened and exhausted, particularly if they are juggling more demands outside of work than their male colleagues (and their partner/spouse, which is often the case). And the truth is that women simply hold less power and political clout in many work contexts, one result being that women with female mentors are less likely to achieve promotion and more likely to leave their jobs than women with male mentors.

3

The Reluctant Male

Why Men Avoid Mentoring Women

Recently graduated from one of the nation's top journalism schools, Rachel was ecstatic when she was hired as an assistant producer at a local television station. Eager to succeed in her new profession, she quickly reached out to peers—female and male—to network. Although her peers were helpful in explaining the day-to-day ins and outs of the station, it soon became clear Rachel needed guidance and support from someone more experienced in the field.

After a few months on the job, it was painfully obvious to Rachel that she wasn't getting opportunities to work on key projects—high-profile stories that could showcase her potential—like several of her male peers. It was evident that her male colleagues were getting more face time and forming connections with the producers (who also happened to be male). Frustrated, Rachel reached out to the only female producer at the station, even though she was in a different department. Although polite, this producer appeared overworked and distracted. She did not reciprocate Rachel's efforts to initiate a mentorship, leaving Rachel feeling snubbed and dejected.

Gentlemen, the evidence shows that Rachel's scenario is all too common. Talented women with sterling credentials and great motivation simply don't get the opportunity to shine like their male peers. Although it's easy to blame the senior woman for failing to assume a mentoring role with Rachel, we have a more pressing concern: where the hell were the men—those senior male producers—who were perfectly situated to "see" Rachel's talent and champion her work? Worse, did they see her potential and *choose* not to mentor her? Too often, men are simply missing in action when it comes to demonstrating inclusive support of women in the workplace. Research evidence confirms this trend. More than half (64 percent) of senior men (vice president level and above) are reluctant to be seen meeting alone with a junior woman.[1] The reasons for this hesitancy and timidity are myriad. In this chapter, we confront the issue of male reluctance to mentor women. We ask that you approach this chapter with humility and introspection. We need you to think honestly about why we of the male persuasion often avoid pushing women forward in the workplace.

Sheryl Sandberg, author of *Lean In*, recently observed that "searching for a mentor has become the professional equivalent of waiting for Prince Charming...women are told that if they can just find the right mentor, they will be pushed up the ladder and whisked away to the corner office to live happily ever after."[2] Sadly, this advice often amounts to little more than a fairy tale for many women. Too often, we—guys—can't relate to a woman's personal experience and professional dilemmas in the workplace. And of course, it is harder to serve as role models for navigating work life if our experiences at work have been quite different. Effective role modeling requires some empathy. If men don't work deliberately at discovering and appreciating women's unique professional and personal concerns, we might just feel inadequate or ineffective in the mentor role. And hey, what guy wants to feel impotent?

Sometimes, both the direct lessons and implicit messages about women transmitted to us by fathers, peers, and our broader culture simply turn out to be bogus. As boys growing up we may have learned that girls are nice but weak, nurturing but too thin-skinned to compete in male-centric organizations. Even in the twenty-first century, when many of us had moms who worked full-time jobs, we may have internalized the stereotype that women just don't have the right stuff for leadership and management positions. Although erroneous, these stereotypes can operate unconsciously to reinforce perceptions that women aren't worthy of our time as mentors.

While most guys don't consciously perpetuate such stereotypes, research reveals that they are indeed alive and well in a host of workplace actions, including hiring and promotion. For instance, a study from the world of music performance demonstrated that when symphony orchestra auditions were conducted using a blind format for the evaluators, there was a 50 percent increase in the number of women offered positions.[3] Other studies using hiring applications and performance evaluations—identical except for the gender of a candidate's name—show that women's performance is evaluated more negatively than men's.[4] The negative impact on women of stereotypes in hiring and promotions is sobering; these decisions impact financial outcomes and upward mobility in the organization.

If men in positions of power in the business world manifest dismissive attitudes toward women, surely women will be more warmly received in the relatively liberal world of higher education, right? Turns out, the answer is no.[5] In a compelling study of gender bias in graduate school, potential doctoral students sent e-mails to graduate school professors—both male and female—across all academic disciplines explaining their common research interests, seeking entry to their doctoral program, and requesting a short meeting with the professor. The professors' response rates provided insight into how bias and discrimination work for those seeking mentorship in their chosen profession. With the exception of the fine arts, women were less likely to receive a response from professors of either gender, regardless of the representation of women in the discipline. And to show the connection to power, prestige, and influence, professors in disciplines where salaries are highest (e.g., business, engineering) and in private universities were the *least* likely to respond to a potential female mentee. Women seeking mentorship in business schools were more than twice as likely as their male counterparts to be ignored by a professor. As men, we can be susceptible to bias and gender stereotypes that cause us to overlook or actively avoid talented women such as the women in this research study. Ask yourself this: How many women and men do you currently mentor? Do these numbers reflect the actual gender ratio in your workplace? If not, why?

In Rachel's story, some of the male producers may have overlooked Rachel because they saw her as the female producer's responsibility. These men cling to the myth that only women can mentor other women. Such archaic thinking may be the product of male socialization, which often paints women as an altogether different—even alien—species. This perception is often associated with a superficially positive notion that women need to be provided for, protected, and revered—*benevolent sexism*. Benevolent sexists cling to the myth that women are fragile, delicate, mysterious creatures that we, mortal men, could not possibly begin to understand, let alone guide and support. Fellas, we have to see through these insidious attitudes if we are going to be successful mentors.

And of course, there are other reasons that men are reluctant to mentor women. Frankly, many of us are simply anxious about engaging in close relationships with women. Referred to as the *developmental dilemma* for male mentors to female mentees, this dilemma describes the tension between wanting to help and develop junior women on one level (a pull toward closeness) and the competing desire to avoid attraction, intimacy, and the complications they can create (a push toward distance). Depending on our experience with opposite-sex relationships, some of us may feel flat-out uncomfortable in a cross-gender mentoring relationship at work. Too many guys don't know how to "do" nonsexual intimacy in relationships with women. We may have no problem being friends and bros with our male peers, but the prospect of being "just friends" with women leaves us off kilter. On one end of the continuum, we fear *sexploitation*, perhaps responding to increasing intimacy with sexual overtures. On the other end of the continuum, we anxiously avoid the very intimacy necessary for developing trust, thereby creating sterile and distant mentorships. Acknowledging our discomfort in collegial but nonsexual relationships with women is a first step. Remember this: our female mentees are not looking for sexual intimacy; they want to develop and succeed, personally and professionally. If we acknowledge our discomfort and then work on mastering it, and if we rule out even the possibility of a sexual relationship with any mentee, we'll be better able to put aside our fear of intimacy and get busy championing the Athenas around us.

Here is another obstacle to male–female mentorships at work. Some men resort to "old scripts" when interacting with women. These men resort to relationship patterns made familiar and comfortable in relationships with other women in their lives, namely, mothers or daughters.

Although this may seem like a good idea, and in fact it may be very helpful in overcoming anxiety, being a woman's "son" or "father" can stymie a developmental relationship with her for several reasons. First, it may lead to "chivalrous" behavior that amounts to little more than benevolent sexism. Responding to women as dependent and fragile leads to overprotection; it will ultimately sabotage their development. Evidence suggests that when women are exposed to this variety of sexism, they begin to doubt their abilities and their likelihood for success.[6] Second, familial relationships are not often conducive to providing the type of brutally honest and direct feedback a woman needs in a competitive workplace. Finally, such "fathering" by a mentor can feel patronizing and smothering to a woman. Using the power dynamic in your mentoring relationship with a woman to rescue, overprotect, and undermine her independence is the last thing she needs. She's not your daughter: remember that!

Still other men are reluctant to mentor women for fear of social scrutiny. How many times have you heard the saying "Perception *is* reality"? Unfortunately, whether we like it or not and whether it is fair or not, perceptions matter. At times, they matter so much that men are reluctant even to consider engaging women in strong developmental relationships. A recent news item about female congressional staffers on Capitol Hill revealed that women are often barred from time alone with their bosses for fear that the male congressman will be "tainted" by innuendo about an affair.[7] Research evidence shows that women are less likely to report engaging in after-work social activities with their male mentors. As Sheryl Sandberg observed, a senior man and a junior man in a bar is seen as mentoring. A senior man and a junior woman at a bar *could* also be mentoring, but... let's face it, it could be much more.[8]

If you fear gossip and raised eyebrows because you are mentoring a woman, you aren't alone. Too many men worry that if they appear strongly supportive or emotionally connected with a woman at work, someone will launch a juicy rumor or write them up for something inappropriate. Worse, a jealous coworker might spread a rumor about an untoward relationship to undermine your mentee! When General Becky Halstead was a junior officer, she often felt the gaze of her coworkers when she worked as an aide for a senior male general. She often worried about how their relationship was being perceived: "Are they getting too close, how do they talk to each other? Everyone just watches you. You get watched more closely than if it's a male general with a male aide." Guys, people talk. You probably can't prevent it entirely, but by mentoring both women and men actively and transparently, you'll contribute to setting the standard for what intentional mentoring across gender should look like.

Gentlemen, let's be frank: sometimes gossip sprouts from a kernel of truth. If you have anxiety about how others will read your relationship with a female mentee, it may be time to ask yourself why that is. Is it rare for you to mentor a woman? If the answer is yes, then your first mentorships with women will naturally generate greater scrutiny. Use this attention to check yourself and your relationship. Be certain that you're *not* giving them something to talk about. Be purposeful about when and where you meet with your mentee. Meeting during normal business hours, on a routine basis, and in a typical meeting place can keep people from getting the wrong idea about your relationship. In most organizations, there is nothing inappropriate about meeting alone with your mentee, as long as you're not making it look like you're trying to hide something. For instance, meeting in the break room, local café, or your company's cafeteria where coworkers are walking by provides a sense of normality that will make everyone more comfortable; candlelight dinners and drinks at trendy bars, not so much.

It is important for men to be cautious about perceptions without going overboard. Excessive worry creates distance in the mentoring relationship. Simply aiming for open, transparent conduct in all your developmental relationships is key. Consider one male manager who described his approach this way: "Whether it's a man, a woman, or a Martian sitting across the desk, I'm not going to treat them any differently. I'm not going to shut the door, I'm not going to be seen showing favoritism. You might call that subconscious risk mitigation."[9] If you mentor women often, if you mentor them professionally and with integrity, and if mentoring talented people of both genders is a hallmark of your identity as a leader, we guarantee you won't have to worry about misperceptions for long.

Here is another factor that can fuel male reluctance to mentor women: the jealous spouse. When men avoid mentoring women, we sometimes hear this concern: "What will my spouse/partner think?" In a perfect world, we would all enjoy ideal relationships with spouses characterized by unflinching trust. But, alas, jealousy and suspicion are part of the human condition. And let's cut our partners some slack. After all, our ancestors were required to fight off romantic rivals as a matter of survival! These instincts and reactions are simply hardwired. Gentlemen, transparency and familiarity are your friends; wise male mentors create opportunities for their spouse or partner to meet and get to know their female mentees.

In our interview with General Becky Halstead, she revealed that as a mentee she was intentional in doing this with her senior male mentors' wives. She found that reaching out to mentors' wives at social occasions helped her mentors and their spouses develop a sense of trust and comfort with the close mentoring relationship and the frequent travel requirements. She said that she always considered the relationship with spouses: "Some wives cannot handle it, some can. The way that I dealt with that challenge was that I did my very best to nurture the relationship with the spouse. The spouse knew who I was as a person and as an officer." Gentlemen, once your partner knows your mentee as a person, and knows that your relationship is professional and important for her career (and yours), you will sleep much better.

Finally, in an age when sexual harassment and equal opportunity complaints are a costly reality to organizations of all stripes, some men are reluctant to mentor women for fear that they will "slip" and say or do something offensive. Anxiety and fear are often perpetuated by rumors of men who are prosecuted by HR for complimenting a woman on her dress. No one wants to get into hot water at work, but increased focus on sexual harassment training to the point where men are scared to interact with female coworkers has led some to describe a new phenomenon at work dubbed the "sex partition."[10] Some men erroneously believe the solution to this risk is avoiding women altogether. Avoiding women in any organization is nonproductive and can be especially damaging in male-dominated organizations, because women have fewer options for mentors.

In fact, male mentors can learn to recognize these dilemmas. An example of this can be found at the quality of life services and facilities management company Sodexo, where a formal mentoring program helps senior male mentors learn to manage their anxiety and biases, thanks to their mentees' feedback.[11] Women participating in the program have been promoted at higher rates than other high-potential women.[12] Successful mentoring relationships rely on open and honest two-way communication. Mentors who foster an environment that encourages feedback and openness will create a relationship where inadvertent "slights" or "slips" can be handled within the relationship and with a purpose of learning from each other. If you make a mistake, admit it, own it! Show that you care for your mentee and she will do the same for you.

Gentlemen, it really is simple. Treat everybody with respect and conduct yourself with dignity, and you will have little to worry about. All the evidence suggests that men can have personally meaningful and professional mentoring relationships with women. To do this, wise mentors establish appropriate boundaries in cross-gender friendships and mentorships.

Don't be a reluctant male. Get over your anxiety about mentoring women. Mentor women deliberately and transparently. The only way to help your organization achieve genuine gender equality and become competitive for the long haul is for you to be *that guy*, the one willing to champion the careers of those rising Athenas around you.

4

The Biology and Psychology of Men and Women in Relationships

Becoming a Thoughtful Caveman

Gentlemen, it's time to address the elephant in the room—*are* men and women really from different planets? Or, does that singular chromosomal distinction between us actually suggest that we are far more alike than different as representatives of the same *Homo sapiens* species? Most scientists agree that the jury is still out on many of the questions about sex differences and why men and women are often differentiated by distinct habits of behavior, including those that manifest at work. Sure, guys are often preoccupied—even mesmerized—by the female body, but the truth is that the elements and qualities that distinguish us from female members of our species are far more nuanced and complicated than breasts and vaginas. In this chapter, we briefly explore the evolutionary, biological, and psychological evidence bearing on the way men and women perceive and relate to each other. We encourage you to appreciate your primitively evolved inclinations vis-à-vis women as well as those deeply socialized messages about how women and men should "be" in relation to one another. In the end, we ask that you become a more thoughtful caveman, an evolved gentleman with the self-awareness and motivation to mentor women well.

RELATIONSHIP BIOLOGY 101

Certainly, some sex differences are—at least in part—biologically determined. For instance, height, muscle composition, body fat, and metabolism tend to consistently differentiate men from women. But merely focusing on these differences may cloud the fact that there is as much difference *within* the sexes as there is *between* the sexes for each of these characteristics. And there is more: many well-established differences between the sexes, such as life expectancy and vulnerability to both physical and psychological illness, are clearly determined by far more than mere biology. For example, throughout history and across cultures, life expectancy is longer for women. Why? Well, there are genetic explanations related to men's chromosomal vulnerability—sorry, guys, there are limitations to that Y chromosome of yours.[1] Additionally, there are social and behavioral explanations that disadvantage the male variety of our species. These include: work stress, lack of social network support, risky behavior, aggression and violence, smoking, alcohol, diet, lack of exercise, and lack of routine medical care.[2] As you can see, clear-cut explanations for most sex differences are not easy to come by. Most male–female differences involve an intricate cocktail of biological, social, and psychological ingredients.

SEX DIFFERENCES AND THE BRAIN

Although the musician Cyndi Lauper once famously reflected, "I don't think men grow a brain until twenty-six or even thirty," it appears men *do* have brains early in life, and in most ways, those brains are remarkably similar to those of their female counterparts. The past decade has witnessed renewed interest in neuroscience and brain development, providing a scientific window into the ways women and men compare at the level of the brain. Neuroscientific research clearly shows small differences in the human brain based on sex, but not the large, consistent differences needed to support the dimorphic view of a "male brain" and a "female brain."[3] For instance, brain scans using functional magnetic resonance imaging (fMRI) reveal unique patterns of activity in male and female brains as well as patterns common to both.[4] In addition, there are small structural differences and variations in patterns of processing neurochemicals between men and women. Finally, we see modest gender differences in cognitive abilities such as spatial visualization (men are slightly better) and working memory (women are slightly better). Even small differences in brain structure and function can contribute to our understanding of subtle distinctions in the way men and women respond and relate to each other. For instance, when mentoring women, men would be well served to appreciate the average female's neurologically rooted tendencies to absorb and retain more sensorial and emotive information, be verbally expressive in connecting memories and current events, and be more analytical of relational feelings.[5] As interesting as these findings may be, they offer little evidence for any profound neurological distinctions between the sexes.[6]

And keep in mind that even these well-established gender patterns in the neuroscientific literature must be interpreted in light of social stereotypes. For example, two consistent gender differences, multitasking and emotionality—typically attributed to biological differences—are in part connected to different life contexts for men and women.

Recently there has been discussion in the media suggesting that women are better than men at multitasking and that women multitask more often (men tend to be more single-task focused). The reality is that there is inconclusive evidence that either men or women are *better* at multitasking; both genders show diminished performance when asked to multitask.[7] But, women do multitask more often than men, which may be more a product of their work–family situation—the greater number of daily demands to attend to at work and at home—than evolution or biology.[8]

A similar pattern emerges with respect to emotionality. Brain scans show that both sexes respond to pictures that should evoke a negative emotion.[9] But there are differences between the sexes at the level of the brain in the capacity to regulate and control feelings.[10] Men appear to be more efficient at regulating emotion, using less neural activity; women are better at reframing negative emotions into positive feelings.[11]

What about tears and crying? A recent study from the Netherlands revealed that on average women cry between thirty and sixty-four times per year compared to seventeen for men.[12] And when they cry, women cry for an average of six minutes while men tear up for only two to three minutes. The reasons for this gender discrepancy are both hormonal and social. Women have higher levels of prolactin, a hormone produced by the pituitary gland associated with emotion, including tears. And women are raised with more social permission to cry; they are less likely to feel ashamed of tears than men.

Is this neuroscientific evidence particularly important for the practice of mentoring? Think of it as simply one element contributing to the gendered differences you may discover in your relationships with women at work.

MAYBE DARWIN WAS ONTO SOMETHING

Guys, let's now consider a more evolutionary perspective on our cavemen heritage. The evidence shows that we are hardwired as men (and women to a lesser degree) to pick up on subtle attraction cues. As men, we consciously and unconsciously *see* women differently than they *see* us. As guys, we unconsciously sense and instantly process the smell of women's pheromones (neurochemicals) and it turns out that—based on smell alone—women mysteriously become more attractive to us when they are most fertile.[13] Beyond smell, physical attraction is often related to facial features and body shape.[14] As it turns out, evolutionary psychology might validate Meghan Trainor's song that it's "All About That Bass." As the theory goes, men are attracted to women who are good mates: sexually mature, youthful, and healthy.[15] This translates into particular body types and features (a 0.7 waist-to-hip ratio is preferred by men in many populations) and facial features (bilateral symmetry, small chin, and thick lips).[16]

Even the very nature of the way we as men take in and process a woman's appearance has roots in our evolution as human males on the hunt for prospective mates. It turns out that we tend to instantly analyze a woman perceptually using *local cognitive processing*. In essence, our inner caveman first glances at a woman's body parts and shape, allowing us to perceive and evaluate her physical potential as a mate.[17] Of course, if you don't have good self-awareness about this evolved tendency, or if your inner caveman gets stuck at an earlier stage of evolution, you might just be that leering, inappropriate male, guilty of overtly objectifying women at work. And to make matters even less fair for women, evidence suggests that guys are not subjected to such visual strip searches by the women they encounter. Instead, men tend to be perceived using *global cognitive processing*, meaning that guys tend to be seen in their entirety, not merely on the basis of their abs, buns, or facial symmetry.

So gentlemen, we know what you're thinking right about now: if some elements of attraction are hardwired, vestiges of our evolved male brains, what are the implications for our relationships with women at work? *Can* men and women just be friends? More important, can men enjoy close, supportive mentoring relationships with women… without sexualizing them or violating boundaries? The answer is an unequivocal *yes*! As a matter of fact, it happens every day. In part 2 of this guide, you'll hear from lots of women about men who championed, supported, and encouraged them without once making the mentorship feel romanticized or creepy.

So, how can you be a guy—a dude with a caveman past—*and* mentor women professionally and platonically? Let's start with rule number 1: remain accepting but alert to your evolved attraction triggers. Gentlemen, we ignore our neurological and biological past at our own peril. Accept the fact that you'll find many women attractive, including some you mentor. No shame here. All heterosexual men are inclined to respond to both general fertility markers and more subtle cues for attraction in women, at least occasionally. Frankly, life might be just a bit duller and less interesting were this not the case. The real problem is that far too many men try to pretend they are not vulnerable to feelings of attraction. Freud observed that denial is the most primitive defense mechanism. But denial of erotic or romantic feelings is often a recipe for disaster. A man in denial of his feelings and attractions puts his female mentee and the value of a mentoring relationship in jeopardy.

Rule number 2: your brain comes with a frontal lobe, so use it! Guys, the frontal portion of your cortex is that highly evolved brain region critical for decision making, judgment, self-regulation, and the inhibition of impulses. Think of it as the brake linings of the brain. Might you be wired with caveman radar that causes you to respond to some women with erotic interest or romantic stirrings? Of course, and you should admit it, understand it, then take responsibility for those responses and prevent them from derailing a good mentorship. If you've come equipped with a frontal lobe, and if it hasn't been seriously damaged, then the neural leftovers from your primitive caveman past are no excuse for sexualizing relationships with women at work. This sort of capitulation to biological impulse was evident when Billy Crystal's character, in the movie *When Harry Met Sally*, reflected that "men and women can't be friends because the sex part always gets in the way."

Here is a third rule: chances are strong that she's just not that into you. Research reveals that men are more likely than women to assume there may be romantic interest in an opposite-sex professional relationship. If we listen uncritically to the evolutionary murmur in our heads, we may erroneously interpret her friendly and collegial behavior as romantic interest and availability.[18] Gentlemen, let us spare you some embarrassment. Research in the area of attraction shows that when men are attracted to women, they often overestimate the extent to which the attraction is mutual.[19] Chances are very good that when you feel attracted to a woman at work, she is not equally enamored of you.

In summary, men *can* and, in fact, *must* have professional, mentoring relationships with women. Thoughtful male mentors are self-aware and nondefensive about their attraction triggers. They are also intentional about preserving good boundaries in their mentoring relationships. When feelings of attraction arise, they are careful to channel them in a healthy way, seek consultation from a trusted colleague, or take other steps to prevent their feelings from intruding on the important work of mentorship. In part 2 of the book, we provide specific strategies to level the evolutionary playing field and keep feelings of attraction in check.

RELATIONSHIP PSYCHOLOGY

Although evidence from evolutionary and biological research on gender and attraction provides important insights about our relationships with women, we now shift our focus to the evidence on the equally powerful effects of gender socialization. *Gender role socialization* is the social process by which men and women learn their social roles at work and home through specific sex-typed tasks and behaviors in the broader culture.[20] All human beings bring their relationship histories and cultural experiences to a mentorship. We learn how to perform important gender roles as boys and girls from a young age from the most influential people in each stage of our lives (e.g., parents, friends, coaches, teachers, clergy, and media).[21] Gender norms and stereotypes are culturally powerful yet most of us would struggle to explain why or how we acquired our socialized beliefs about appropriate gendered behavior. We'll start with a few of the socialized roles women often learn.

Sugar and Spice and Everything Nice

Think about a woman you work with and know well. Ever wonder why she won't just tell people directly what she wants them to do, or why she spends so much time talking to others about what they think or how they feel, or do you wonder why she won't make a decision quickly and move out smartly?! Like guys, women are socialized to enact certain roles in relationships, even if some of these roles and behaviors reinforce stereotypes. For instance, many of the women you mentor may have been socialized to accept that women should: hesitate to ask for what they want; avoid appearing too confident or showing up their male peers; avoid conflict by glossing over rude, chauvinistic, abusive male behavior; work to please; deny discomfort or anger; choose between being attractive or smart; and always cooperate, never compete. Here is an important caveat, gentlemen: these are norms and not absolutes—not every woman you mentor will adhere to the same gendered behavior. So you'll have to get to know each of your mentees as a unique person and individual woman, and not make assumptions. Finally, gentlemen, be sensitive to the previous experiences women have had with men generally and their male guides specifically without pushing inappropriately for specifics about the experiences. Wait for her to share anything about her previous relationships with men that might be important in understanding her.

Snips and Snails and Puppy Dog Tails

Men must also be self-aware when it comes to our own "scripts" (courtesy of our families and masculine socialization generally) for how to be in relationships with women. Like women, men are socialized in ways that emphasize behavioral norms and stereotypes associated with masculinity. For instance, men are often socialized by parents, peers, and the broader culture to: overlook women at work (we fail to see them as potential leaders); embody the protector archetype (we overprotect women, and in so doing undermine their autonomy); and attempt to express intimacy sexually (we can feel uncomfortable with navigating intimacy in a nonphysical way).[22] These behavioral inclinations toward women play out in the performance of our roles at work and will undoubtedly influence the way we perform as mentors to women. So, which socialized behavioral pattern with women best describes you? Guys, let's take a look at some of the most common relationship scripts men are socialized to enact, and how each can help—or impede—our ability to mentor women well.

As a guy, you can probably relate to this scenario at work: you are interacting with a younger woman and catch yourself wondering how she is interpreting your behavior and language. Perhaps you don't know her well, you haven't had many working relationships with younger women, or you simply feel unsure or uncertain about what is appropriate. Most importantly, you don't want to do anything wrong or make a mistake that will offend her because, after all, you're a guy with good intentions. As humans, we don't like to get it wrong in our social interactions; we're embarrassed when we do. Naturally, we draw on the most accessible road maps to navigate interpersonal exchanges, hoping to avoid a wreck! The most accessible relational maps are the scripts we have learned from previous relationships with women, often family members, siblings, or intimate partners. Our socialized man scripts for interacting with women help to reduce our anxiety in times of uncertainty. The problem, of course, is that these old scripts may not be valid or productive when it comes to your female mentee. Gentlemen, you wouldn't let your car's GPS maps get outdated, so why would you navigate relationships with women using guidance from decades past? Let's look at some of the most common relationship scripts men have often internalized.

Many men may easily enact dependency scripts with women, seeking "mothering" in soothing and nurturing behaviors from the women we become close to at work. Others of us are quick to embody the big brother or father role with women, rushing in to protect and shelter them when what they really need is simple affirmation and encouragement. The protector role is quite natural and healthy for a parent and child; it is something quite different when a male mentor rushes in to protect a female mentee at every turn. Protection easily becomes overprotection, and it is guaranteed to undermine your female mentee by preventing her from learning to manage the risk and challenges of organizations on her own.[23] Even if a mentee appears content to accept your fatherly protection, remember that she, too, has been socialized to enact scripts (e.g., daughter). Do your mentee a favor and don't try to be her dad. Your mentee needs you to be her mentor.

Another version of the protector script in male–female relationships is the "chivalrous knight" and the "helpless maiden."[24] According to this script, the mentor is strong and competent while the mentee lacks skills and abilities to survive in the workplace. She must overrely on her mentor and assume the subordinate role in the relationship. Instead of fostering a collegial adult relationship, this script serves to reinforce a power discrepancy in the mentoring relationship. Remember that our role as mentors is to develop our mentees so they can advance to become valued colleagues in our network. When guys get stuck playing chivalrous knight and overprotecting women at work, they paradoxically prevent their mentees from becoming full, independent members of the profession.

As men, the chivalrous knight script comes all too naturally. As boys, we often learned to be independent, self-reliant, tough, and stoic. The protective knight script requires us to be emotionless and rational, despite the fact that all the mentoring research shows that excellent mentors are authentic and emotionally responsive to their mentees' needs. Guys, take our word for it and leave the stoic warrior role for King Leonidas.

The final script is the most toxic and genuinely risky for the women you mentor. Strong mentoring relationships are innately intimate. But when intimacy triggers enactment of "macho" and "seductress" role scripts, the mentoring relationship is often doomed.[25] This script warps a relationship so that the mentee's career development or aspirations get lost in a haze of flirtation and sexual innuendo. Seductive behavior in a mentorship creates an atmosphere where developing competence is no longer the focus and the mentee may feel trapped in an unproductive and unwanted relationship.

In one train wreck after another, we have seen otherwise successful men scuttle their careers and do real harm to women whom they were ostensibly guiding by resorting to sexual relationship scripts as a means of managing feelings of attraction and the experience of intimacy in a friendship with a woman at work. Again, seductiveness and physical connection are often linked to our earlier experiences and wishes vis-à-vis women. This script may be most dangerous when a man is unaware that he is enacting it, perhaps until long after it is too late. This is dangerous territory because it can lead to behavior that qualifies as sexual harassment. Do yourself a favor and leave the sexual intimacy at home. And remember the research, guys: she's not that into you anyway...

We all have well-learned, sometimes implicit and unconscious scripts for how to be in relationships with women. Problems occur when we are unaware of them and they run amok in our mentorships, undermining strong collegial relationships with the women in our lives. Want to be an excellent mentor? Then learn and understand the biological, psychological, and social influences that have made you who you are. Only a deliberate and self-aware man can have the insight to mentor women in a healthy and productive relationship. We know you are up to the task!

5

A Few Good Men

Why Men Should Mentor Women Well

January 30, 2016, Fort Sill, Oklahoma, "Home of Marine Artillery"

Second Lieutenant Virginia Brodie, United States Marine Corps, coated with a patina of dusty sweat, surveys the barren firing range where she is learning to be a Marine artillery officer. A recent graduate of the Marine Corps' grueling indoctrination training for all incoming officers at The Basic School (TBS) in Quantico, Virginia, she now stands on the precipice of becoming the first female officer in a combat military occupational specialty (MOS). Virginia's path to Fort Sill was filled with challenges and hurdles that tested her physically, mentally, and emotionally, but soon she will achieve her goal of leading Marines—in a combat unit.

Virginia's presence at Fort Sill is improbable. To begin, she is a woman, one of only two from her Basic School class selected to break the gender barrier in Marine Corps Artillery. And 2nd Lt. Brodie is not the most physically formidable Marine you may ever have encountered. Virginia stands five feet and two and a half inches tall. And despite the grueling conditions around her, she disarms others immediately with a beaming smile. Today, in a rare quiet moment between field exercises while eating an MRE (Meal Ready to Eat), Virginia laughs, remembering that it wasn't until her Plebe Summer at the U.S. Naval Academy that she really understood how much smaller she was compared to many of her male peers. Looking at a picture of her squad during a physical training exercise, straining to carry a log pole, she finds it hard to believe that she stands barely at chest level of the young men on either side of her. But 2nd Lt. Brodie has never let her physical stature deter her.

As she reflects on the people who inspired, affirmed, prepared, and championed her to be one of the first women ever to enter the ranks of Marine Artillery, Virginia is acutely aware that her success is due to more than her own grit and singular determination; her success is also due to more than the good favor of Saint Barbara, Patron Saint of Artillery. In Virginia's mind, her success is also due to men who have mentored her at critical moments along the way.

Virginia's dad conveyed consistent affirmation, convincing her that she was capable and competent, and that her size need never hinder her aspirations. When word trickled through the ranks at TBS that all combat jobs might soon be open to women, Virginia remembers her excitement just thinking about leading Marines in a combat unit. Rather than dismiss her vision, Virginia's TBS classmate Payton motivated her to go on ten-mile runs and repeatedly practice the obstacle course. Payton affirmed her vision by holding her to his same high standard. Although painful at the time, his tough support helped prepare her to excel as a Marine. Many of Virginia's male officers and professors at the Naval Academy were also vital in fanning her confidence in herself as a competent leader. And her rowing coach made it abundantly clear that she was the finest varsity boat coxswain on the Severn River, no matter her size or gender.

More recently, during her time at TBS, Virginia remembers her delight listening to the Secretary of Defense announce on December 3, 2015, that all military positions would be open to women. This was followed shortly by disappointment and discouragement when she was informed that the Marine Corps could require years to implement the change. What happened? Two male Marine Corps officers in Virginia's chain of command decided to push hard to let Virginia select a combat arms MOS. She reflects that, were it not for their advocacy, that might have been the end of her dream. These strong male mentors saw Virginia's potential as a leader; they demonstrated unflinching confidence in her potential as a Marine artillery officer. They stuck their boots through the men-only career door to ensure Virginia wouldn't be rejected at the gate.

At Fort Sill, before heading out to the next field exercise, Virginia breaks into that beaming smile at the thought of her journey. She is thinking how lucky she is—yet it has nothing to do with luck or good fortune, just a small Marine's tenacity and a few good mentors.

You want answers? You want the truth? As strong, thoughtful men, you can handle the truth! The evidence is in, gentlemen. When men mentor women, those women make more money, enjoy more promotions, receive greater acceptance from other men in the workplace, and are more satisfied with their careers—and, most important, mentored women are far more likely to remain loyal to the organization in which they are mentored.[1] Organizations and institutions around the globe are waging war to recruit, retain, and advance women in the workplace. Firms with more women in top positions simply perform better.[2]

Traditionally masculine "command and control" structures of hierarchical management are yesterday's news. Leaders imposing their will upon followers, employing a "just do as I say" style of leadership, are frankly passé. Individual task accomplishment is, in the Internet age, rapidly being replaced with more team-based and group-focused projects.[3] Organizations today demand social intelligence, creativity, and the capacity to develop transformational relationships with peers and followers—the very skills and traits often correlated with feminine approaches to leadership.[4] Although women want to be included fully in the workplace, one recent comprehensive study found that 82 percent of women felt excluded at work, even though 92 percent of their male coworkers didn't think they were excluding women.[5] Houston, we have a problem: clearly there is a disconnect in the way men and women experience inclusivity at work. In a dire warning about the battle for inclusivity in the workplace, former CEO of Sodexo Dick Macedonia shared this in our recent interview with him: "We are in a battle for talent. And let's be clear that talent does not have a gender. If we don't get the very best people into our organization and into the right jobs—no matter what they look like—we will suboptimize our organization. This could be an issue of business survival. Inclusivity is a business imperative." Organizations that don't get this right are in real trouble.

IF NOT ME(N), THEN WHO?

As a minority group in many organizations—always at risk of being marginalized—women encounter unique challenges and barriers to finding mentors, compared with their male counterparts.[6] For this reason, intentional male mentors can be even more powerful and pivotal for women. Though often told, "Go find a mentor," women in real life may not find it so easy to follow this advice. When a younger woman seeks guidance and initiates interaction with a more senior man in her organization, she may feel intimidated by his status or worried how her overtures for time and attention will be interpreted. She might worry that the prospective mentor—not to mention her peers—will speculate that she's interested in *more* than mentoring, perhaps trying to sleep her way to the top. Rarely would one of her male peers ever have to worry about this misperception.

This is where guys have got to step in. Rather than let women flounder in an environment with few senior women, we, men, must recognize talented women and then become deliberate mentors for them. This is clearly best for junior women, but let's be perfectly frank, it is also best for our organizations and ourselves. Listen to how 2nd Lt. Virginia Brodie describes the way one of her excellent male mentors did this: "He believed in me and saw the potential that I didn't know that I had. He was such a great help and to this day I still go to him for advice and get a different perspective. I give him all the credit for me going to the Naval Academy because he was definitely the catalyst. He worked with the academy and put me on a pedestal for them to see why they really needed me. He's been a very good role model and mentor for me."

Evidence from decades of research shows that powerful male–female mentorships are far more likely to be initiated by the mentor, or mutually initiated by both parties.[7] The evidence is clear: men are uniquely positioned in many organizations to set the tone for inclusivity in the workplace. Guys do this when they intentionally sponsor the most talented men *and* women. Powerful male mentors don't wait. They purposefully identify promising women in their organization and reach out, initiating interaction and support without being asked. Virginia Brodie would not be a Marine artillery officer if it was not for a few good men recognizing her talent and championing her all the way. These officers had the insight and vision to see how it would be good for Virginia, but also terrific for the Marine Corps, to keep her in the fight. Most importantly, they had the intestinal fortitude to go to bat for her.

Gentlemen, you don't have to be a Marine to see the talented everyday Athenas in your organization and how they are making a difference. But you *do* have to be that proactive guy who takes initiative for sponsoring talented women in the same way you sponsor talented men. The mentor's interest, initiative, and commitment are critically important and highly correlated with strong career benefits for the female mentee. Women who do find male mentors—especially in traditionally masculine professions and organizations—will later recall "fork-in-the-road stories." They recall encountering a man who declared that they were performing well and capable of much more, and who encouraged them to take on new challenges. These expressions of support and belief were often defining in women's decisions to persist and excel in difficult circumstances. Once again, consider the experience of 2nd Lt. Virginia Brodie; there are no more difficult circumstances than being the first woman to enter an all-male Marine Corps combat artillery unit: "My staff platoon commander was an infantry officer in charge of my platoon and responsible for counseling and career guidance. He was awesome. He actually viewed me just as a Marine. Not a female Marine; not a small, short Marine; just a Marine like any of the other male Marines who wanted to be infantry officers or artillery officers. He saw me as an artillery officer, even though the policy didn't allow that yet."

SHOW HER HOW SHE CAN "BE ALL [SHE] CAN BE"

Excellent mentors for women exude unrelenting confidence in a mentee's potential and her capacity to realize her aspirations. This sort of confidence can offset and override a mentee's self-doubt about whether she's qualified to do the job. While we men are more likely to overestimate our abilities and performance, women tend to *underestimate* their abilities and performance.[8] As we discussed in chapter 2, men do not hesitate to take credit for successes at work, while women are more likely to attribute their success to luck or good fortune.[9] Throughout our interviews with some of the most successful women across all professions, we heard time and time again that they felt "fortunate" or "lucky."

Some women are less willing to put themselves out there and risk applying for those dream jobs, jobs that might be a stretch in terms of experience and qualifications. Guys are socialized to take more risks. We have less fear of failure because we tend to inflate our assessment of our own talents and competence. In the workplace, especially in organizations with mostly guys, women may find it less enticing to take risks in jobs where failure as a woman could reinforce the "prove it again" bias.[10] The truth is that a woman must often contend with the reality that her qualifications and competence are only as good as her last performance. Quite unfairly, men are often given the nod based on our potential. As a mentor, you've got to appreciate why potential failure is a scarier thought for women; as her mentor, you can help offset her reservations with a steady narrative about her real competence and potential.

One component of outstanding mentoring of women involves helping them to decipher your organizations' *man codes*. Sharing insider information such as informal rules, benign and toxic personalities, and behavior likely to get them positive attention is simply good mentorship. For instance, when specific qualifications and requirements are included in a new job description, women are more likely to refrain from applying if they don't meet all the qualifications. Women are socialized from a young age to follow rules and tend to exude more ethical behavior as a result.[11] But a good mentor might inform her that nobody who applies for the job will meet all the qualifications; he might encourage her to throw her hat in the ring anyway if he believes she is ready. As male mentors, we must exude confidence in a woman's ability to succeed within the formal as well as unwritten business rules that we know all too well. What a guy might take for granted in a male-centric organization may turn out to be the key information our female mentee needs to take the next step and land her dream job.

WHAT'S IN IT FOR ME?

Great mentors don't only mentor women because it's good for their mentees and their organizations. Here's a little secret: if you're a guy and an excellent mentor to women, chances are you'll benefit from these relationships too, often in powerful and measureable ways. In the earliest study of mentoring relationships at work, male–female mentoring alliances resulted in synergy, enjoyment, and creative innovations.[12]

Male mentors report broadened work and interpersonal skills through positive relationships with women. Adding female mentees to your network of mentoring relationships will undoubtedly diversify your range of interpersonal skills and make you a more effective leader in your organization. After all, mentoring is an increasingly important management competence. It requires deliberate development. Research clearly shows that mentoring will make you feel better about yourself as a person, help you develop patience, and lead you to feel more effective.[13]

Mentoring studies also reveal that male mentors to women report benefiting in terms of a sense of purpose, as well as in genuine gratification about giving to the next generation of leaders while enhancing their organizations' prospects for success.[14] And there are sometimes more tangible benefits, too. Often, the rich networks of relationships these men develop help them to outperform their peers in earning more promotions and pay raises![15] Those guys with a reputation as excellent developers of talent—female and male—often become known as star makers.[16] And star makers tend to be prized and rewarded by smart leaders for increasing the performance of the organization as well as helping retain top talent.

Finally, mentees often provide their mentors with an excellent and current source of insider information and a fresh perspective about the organization. Because some mentors operate in upper levels of leadership, they can feel detached or insulated from others. Frequent engagement with mentees offers a key connection to lower levels of the organization.

Tangible benefits for male mentors aside, let's reflect on the words of our colleague, Sheryl Sandberg: "It should be a badge of honor for men to sponsor women."[17] We agree. Making the world more equal, being part of the solution, and bringing the unique talents and perspectives of women to bear on the workplace should be reward enough. As if these reasons weren't sufficiently compelling, we ask you to pause and consider the important women in your life. Now, ask yourself whether your sister, wife, or daughter deserves outstanding mentorship to help her realize her potential and dreams—absolutely!

WHO AM I TO ADVOCATE FOR WOMEN?

As author and education leader Kent Keith advises, "If you do good, people will accuse you of selfish ulterior motives—*Do good anyway.*"[18] Guys, we get it. You might be tormenting yourself with the "What Will Everyone Think?" Syndrome. A sudden interest in helping women in your organization may at first feel uncomfortable for you and creepy to others. Your buddies may ask if you've suddenly joined the feminist movement. Been there, done that, got the T-shirt. Without a clear-cut self-interest in mentoring women, you may experience some backlash. Initially, some may not take you seriously and others might question your motives.[19] But the evidence is in: mentoring women is good for women, organizations, and mentors. The alliance of men who support women at work is an alliance we all should belong to.

Like you, we are men and have never experienced being a woman. We don't presume to understand women's lived experiences but we do have a genuine interest in improving our organization and feel a responsibility as social scientists to use the research and evidence available to improve everyone's experiences at work.

So, where do we go from here? Your humble authors advocate for a strengths-based approach to mentoring that neither overemphasizes gender differences nor tries to discount our unique experiences by claiming we're all the same. Instead, we focus on recognizing, leveraging, and maximizing the unique talents, skills, and abilities we all bring to the workplace—no matter our gender. The advantage you will enjoy by being gender inclusive in your mentoring will be recognized in a more cohesive and competitive organization where everyone wins.

WALKING THE WALK

We've titled this chapter "A Few Good Men" for a reason. It takes a confident and courageous man to mentor a woman. It takes a man who won't tolerate gender disrespect or discrimination in the workplace and a guy committed to making his organization competitive for the long haul. You can be *that guy*, the one who "walks the walk" and is instrumental in the development and career success of men and women alike. Sure, there may be some raised eyebrows, startled expressions, and even whispered rumors from time to time, but to this we ask, is that really so terrifying? We think you can hack it. We challenge you to become a champion for women, a man with a flexible, inclusive vision of gender, a man who truly sees gender as irrelevant to choices about profession and career, and a self-aware man who expresses not even a hint of limitation about the potential of the women he encounters or what they can become.

Confused as to how to do this well? Worried that you'll goon it up? Hang in there, because we've got the ultimate set of tools to help you be successful and a manual to go with them—yes, you have to read the directions in the manual this time! If you're ready to answer the call and accept this mission, turn the page and follow us into part 2 of this guide, the manual for mentoring women well. In part 2, we'll show you the nuts and bolts, the true elements of mentoring women.

Onward!

PART II

Mentoring Women

A Manual for Men

6

Preliminaries

Gentlemen, it is time to get started. We've established that—like men—women have a better shot at success when mentored. And in many organizations, women with a male mentor go further and get paid more.[1] Yet, too often women struggle to secure a mentor of either gender,[2] and if they do happen to attract the attention of an accomplished male at work, they may be disappointed by his "bro-oriented" mentoring strategies, strategies that might work for that "dude" down the hall but that ultimately leave her feeling misunderstood, further isolated, or forced to hide her genuine career ambitions and life priorities.

We acknowledge right up front that mentoring women won't always be easy. At times, cross-gender mentorships can be complex and personally taxing. You may discover tensions related to gender stereotypes, your own baggage with women, anxiety about feelings of attraction, public scrutiny, and even occasional resentment or ridicule from your own peers.[3] To this we say, "So what?" Pulling up and pushing forward talented women is the right thing to do. And there's plenty in this for you too. Evidence and experience predict that some of the women you mentor will become wonderful colleagues and loyal allies. Some will become treasured lifelong friends. And let's not forget, men who mentor women well often benefit in the form of raises, promotions, and expanded networks of influence. Smart organizations of all stripes reward their rainmakers and talent developers.

Here are eight foundational elements that serve to anchor your mentorships with women on sturdy footings. First, commit to putting your mentee's best interests first and foremost; mentors own an ethical duty to avoid causing harm to mentees. Excellent mentors for women work at developing self-awareness of their own gender biases and their well-ingrained "man scripts," and they work at preventing these from interfering with their mentoring work. Strong male mentors for women are all in; they take initiative for reaching out to promising women and they are assertive, authentic, and reliable when it comes to advocating for women and gender-fair policies in the workplace. Finally, terrific mentors are humble about what they don't know about women, cautious to avoid assumptions, and open to learning about their individual mentee's unique experiences.

1. First, Do No Harm

Here is your first and foremost responsibility: take care to always promote your mentee's best interests. Never undermine, exploit, or dismiss her. Susan Chambers, Walmart executive vice president, global people division, explained how it felt to be undermined:

> I was given the authority to make a decision for Walmart on how we were going to handle B2B at a time when e-commerce and the Internet were developing. It was challenging to predict what "winning" was going to look like. I brought together a number of people from the outside and I was ready to sign a contract and make a decision. My boss came in to me that morning and said, "I signed the contract and made the decision." He's standing there looking triumphant and happy like I should be very proud of him. I was so angry, I couldn't talk to him. He said, "I don't get it. Why are you so angry?" I said, it was my decision. It wasn't yours. You gave it to me, I have lots of people involved, I was bringing you a recommendation this afternoon, and you decided out of ego or otherwise that you were going to win this, you were going to do it yourself. Later he came back and said he would never do anything like that to me again and acknowledged that he had never realized that trying to solve that issue for the company himself was usurping my authority and the role he had given me.

The original Hippocratic Oath obligated physicians to "abstain from whatever is harmful or mischievous." So, too, must you always mentor women with their welfare and best interests at heart. Think of your mentorships with women as *fiduciary* relationships. Lawyers, doctors, and other professionals have fiduciary obligations to their clients. Ethical professionals accept the trust and confidence of clients and therefore are obligated to act with the utmost good faith and solely for the benefit of those clients. So, too, should you act on behalf of your female mentees. Here is a simple strategy to help you remain true to this element of mentoring: before any important decision in the mentoring relationship, ask yourself, "How exactly is this in *her* best interest?" If the answer isn't immediately apparent, you'd better rethink it.

Perhaps nothing stands to create more havoc in a man's relationships with women than *power*. Most mentorships involve a clear power differential; the mentor—by virtue of rank, position, or tenure in the organization—simply holds more power (e.g., resources, networks, decisional authority) than the mentee. And when mentors are a relatively scarce commodity, then mentees may work hard to appease the mentor, sometimes tolerating negative or exploitive relationships.[4] Even more concerning, many women are quite trusting of male mentors,[5] and mentoring relationships always come with implicit (unspoken) expectations; a mentee may feel that she owes her mentor far more than the mentor owes her.[6] Even if you never convey any expectation of her, be very aware that your mentee's sense of obligation to you may be palpable. This is all the more reason for caution in avoiding emotional enmeshment or romantic involvement. In such power-unequal relationships, never kid yourself into imagining that she can easily say no when you ask her for something. Always be vigilant to honor appropriate boundaries and refrain from any suggestion or request that might carry a hint of exploitation.[7] In the immortal words of Obi-Wan Kenobi, "Use the force [power]"—but only use it to promote her best interests.

Beyond your own awareness of and respect for power dynamics, there are several additional things a male mentor can do to avoid harm to a female mentee. First, clarify your expectations at the outset. The first woman to rise to the rank of admiral in the U.S. Navy, Michelle Howard, recommends that mentors make transparent up front anything their mentee needs to do to participate fully in the mentorship (e.g., collaborate on research projects, accept increasing challenges, communicate any problems or concerns immediately). Second, remember that rank and hierarchy may be unfamiliar and noxious to many women. If you are too power conscious and formal, women may have a tough time relating to you or benefiting from the relationship. Strive for a more egalitarian, relational approach to mentoring;[8] be her friend not her superior. Third, never abandon a mentee. Sure, there may be moments when you feel uncertain how to help her, concerned about public perceptions of your relationship, and perhaps even anxious about your feelings for her.[9] Instead of leaving her in the lurch, perhaps assuming she is to blame or somehow unworthy of your continued support, you need to man up and address your discomfort and anxiety head on. Few things are more disheartening and damaging to a mentee than to have her mentor pull a 180 and duck out. Finally, if you're a guy with a past, by all means, don't let your baggage torpedo your mentee's career. Got enemies in the organization? How about a reputation for a past indiscretion? Do what it takes to protect her from the "contagion" of your own history and political messes.

2. Know Thyself I: Confront Your Gender Biases

Gentlemen, here's the thing: we all—and we do mean *all*—tend to make instantaneous, automatic, often unconscious assumptions about others. We do it every day (e.g., overweight people are just____; Asians are always ____; short men tend to ____). And of course, as men, we easily and quickly label and categorize the other half of the human race based on the effects of a single chromosome. We are all practiced experts at making rapid-fire—and it turns out, often inaccurate—assumptions about the female variety of our species. Think we're exaggerating? Try this: as you read each item below, answer it as quickly as you can. What is the very first thing that comes to mind? Be honest. Go!

Most women are _____.
Females always need _____.
Compared to boys, girls _____.

At work, women just _____.

Female bosses _____.

Now review your responses. Are there a couple that make you cringe? Would sharing them with a group of female colleagues make you blush?

It turns out that if you are a guy, you probably make a number of automatic and deeply biased assumptions about women every day.[10] True, women are sometimes guilty of their own stereotyped assumptions about men, but our focus here is how men's stereotyped beliefs about women can lead to faulty assumptions about the women we mentor. Consider the following gender biases many men harbor. Whether conscious or hidden, subtle or malicious, all of them have the potential to undermine women and poison our mentoring efforts:

- Women lack sufficient drive and career commitment; they don't possess the ambition to make it.
- Women will eventually leave to have children; they're a risky investment.
- Women are overcommitted outside of work; they're too busy being wives and mothers to be productive and get promoted.
- Women who work as many—or more—hours than men are aberrant; they should be home tending to children and spouse.
- Women don't have the leadership traits necessary to succeed; they're not assertive, competitive, or stoic enough.
- Women are too emotional; they lack the mental toughness required to lead.
- Strong women are bitches; strong men are leaders.

We can nearly guarantee that the talented women you mentor will encounter these and other biases daily; the more male-dominated the workplace, the more pervasive the gender bias.

Listen to the experiences of two women who made it to the top. Former Air Force Brigadier General Dana Born recalled that one of her early male supervisors would often ask her advice on key strategic decisions. "I recall that this man would often preface his questions with,

'Unemotionally, what is your take?' He was saying, keep your emotion out of it. But passion about an issue and emotion often blur. When I express myself on an issue I am passionate about, others sometimes perceive it as being emotional." General Born described being pressured to change her entire persona, her way of communicating, both because her boss expected all women to "be emotional" and because he was obviously uncomfortable when emotion entered a conversation. In a similar vein, listen to the experience of Janet Petro, deputy director of the Kennedy Space Center: "Men seem to expect women to be kind, nurturing, and nice. I had a very negative experience with a male colleague who complained I was not 'likeable.' It was all about his bias that if you're a woman who is strong and no nonsense, you're not likeable. I wish men could really understand their own biases and expectations about women."

Here is the worst of it: many of our stereotypes about women operate below conscious awareness.[11] Implicit or unconscious biases are corrosive to good mentorship, not only because she will feel stereotyped and diminished as a colleague, but worse, women sometimes harbor and internalize these stereotypes so that they actually become self-fulfilling prophecies.[12] Even the subtle message you are unconsciously communicating (e.g., she doesn't have what it takes to make it at the next level) may cause her to see herself through that lens. Even if you demonstrate only through behavior—never words—that you privilege the men you mentor with greater favor and opportunity, she'll get the message loud and clear: she's not as worthy. The tragedy here is that women are already socialized to hide their ambitions and aspirations; they learn early to deflect attention from themselves and let the guys around them take credit. As for women's ambitions, like men, they need recognition and acknowledgement of their successes to keep the fires stoked—they're just not as likely to find it. Guys, if you want to mentor well, you've got to face your own biases about the capability and potential of women. Then, you need to start actively getting to know and deliberately sponsoring women at work. Only exposure to talented women and experience pushing them forward will change stereotyped attitudes.

We close with a little top-secret intel, guys: to the extent that you develop a broad, inclusive, flexible view of gender—one driven by fewer myths and stereotyped attitudes about women—you will probably become a more successful husband, father, and friend.[13] Certainly, your children—daughters and sons—need to see you actively affirming and including women. And we have *never* met a woman who reported a negative reaction to her male partner's efforts to better appreciate her experience and support her work–life choices unconditionally.

3. Know Thyself II: Understand Your "Man Scripts"

Think about the women in your life when you were growing up. Did you have sisters? Did you have true friendships with girls, or did they mostly make you feel nervous? Did your mother have a career outside the home? If you grew up with both parents, was your parents' relationship quite traditional or did they share parenting and domestic chores more equally? How did they treat one another? If you have dated women, how would you describe your role in those relationships? Perhaps more important, how would the women you have helped during your career describe you? Are you the warrior/protector, wise father figure, belt-notching seducer, or perhaps just the "best friend" type?

Guys, we are all actors in a play. Throughout our childhood and adolescence, we've been handed scripts that tell us how to enact our roles as men with women. Now, as adults, when we encounter women in the workplace—particularly when women are a minority—we naturally default to these man scripts; they help us to reduce feelings of uncertainty and anxiety that can arise when we work closely with someone of the opposite sex. In her pioneering research on cross-gender mentorship at work, organizational psychologist Kathy Kram found that both sexes quickly assume stereotypical roles in relating to each other.[14] Do they help us work together more effectively? Often, they do not, but they sure can make the dynamics more familiar and help us feel more relaxed!

Think of this as *sex-role spillover*.[15] Men who are uncomfortable with women at work naturally react to them from the perspective of the male/female roles and patterns they are most familiar with in their personal lives (e.g., sex object, lover, wife, daughter, mother). These familiar scripts may be comforting and stabilizing, but they are often irrelevant to work. Sometimes, they are quite harmful. To make matters even more challenging, men and women often collude together in an unconscious dance, enacting familiar scripts that can sabotage a woman at work. Faced with uncertainty, both sexes may unwittingly drag their accustomed ways of interacting with the opposite sex into the here-and-now mentoring relationship. These stereotyped roles spring from our early experience but they also have biological and even evolutionary roots. Make me anxious and put me in an unfamiliar work relationship with a woman, and my caveman brain defaults all too quickly to, "Me Tarzan, you Jane."

Here are three of the most common man scripts.[16] Take an honest look at each of them. Then, ask yourself if any of these patterns feel familiar. Certainly, we can enact more than one script in our mentorships with women.

◆ *Father–Daughter*: Most prevalent and risky when a mentorship involves an older man and a younger woman, the father script guides a man to assume the roles of wise guide and protector. This mentor guides a mentee while shielding her from the risks and struggles of organizational life. If the "father" is unconditionally accepting and communicates approval of the "daughter," this script might work for a time. But the father–daughter script requires a woman to maintain the role of one who is less competent and requires protection. This script too often undermines a mentee's autonomy and it is certain to stifle emergence of a coequal, collegial partnership at work.

◆ *Warrior/Knight–Maiden in Distress*: When a male mentor defaults to a chivalrous knight script, he may unconsciously provoke female mentee scripts such as "helpless maiden." He may see himself as stronger, more competent, and bound by honor to rescue her at every turn. If she plays along with this script, the female mentee may feel pressured—often unconsciously—to hide her own competence or perhaps even pretend neediness or ineptness. Alternatively, she may default to playing nurturing mother to the tough warrior, serving as his confidante and soothing him behind the scenes. Like the father–daughter script, this arrangement is guaranteed to stunt her professional development and limit the growth of the mentorship.

◆ *Seducer–Seductress*: When a man has a strong need to be loved and adored by women, he may enact the script of macho seducer. This mentor may be unconsciously dependent upon female mentees to validate his masculinity and attractiveness.[17] Such mentorships might include flirtation and thinly disguised erotic tension. Although these mentoring scripts may appear fun, even titillating on some level, they nearly always distract attention from a woman's intellectual and professional contributions, and there is a real risk that the male's need for validation and the female's need for intimacy in the relationship may interact in a way that makes a sexual affair—a profound violation of his obligation to do no harm—more likely.

We mention these scripts, not to shame you—we see no value in shame—but to provoke self-awareness and honesty. You didn't choose the scripts you enact with women. Yet somehow, through evolution and early experience, they have been coded on your hard drive. There are several problems with enacting stereotyped man scripts in your mentorships with women.[18] First, each script is likely to reduce your mentee's competence and effectiveness at work. Even if your pattern of behavior is unconscious, responding to a female mentee as a daughter, helpless maiden, or romantic partner serves to entrap her in a role that naturally undermines her ability to separate from the mentor and be taken seriously. Second, each of these traditional gender roles reinforces the power discrepancy in the relationship; she may quickly become mired in a permanently hierarchical mentorship. Finally, each of these scripts will force you, the mentor, to maintain the façade of wise, all-knowing, battle-hardened expert. In so doing, you will miss out on the opportunity to enjoy a two-way relationship, one that contributes to your own personal and professional growth.

Want to mentor women well? Face your man scripts and refuse to let them jeopardize your mentoring relationships with women! First, become more self-aware and explore your own pattern of relating to women generally. Second, spend time with the women you mentor and be deliberate about building a strong friendship; greater trust will reduce the need to resort to stereotyped roles. Finally, if you discover you are enacting any of the scripts mentioned in this element, avoid overreacting and withdrawing abruptly from the mentorship. Manage your own discomfort with intimacy or attraction responsibly. Sudden aloofness and avoidance are never constructive.

4. Be "That" Guy

If you're serious about mentoring women well, if you aspire to be a genuine change agent for women in the workplace, you really have to "be that guy," as Kathy Hannan, partner for diversity and corporate responsibility, KPMGm explained:

> Establish trust with your behavior first. Advocate for her, toot her horn, push her forward, make it clear that you believe in her performance. Start mentoring her before you are formally assigned to this role. Just "be that guy" who does it without being asked. You tell her you believe in her with your behavior and actions. Doing that first creates the trust that leads to a genuine mentorship.

You have to be that guy who really gets it, the one who understands that as women enter leadership positions at work, organizations are more effective and collegial.[19] More women in the workplace translates to greater flexibility, cooperation, and organizational success. And you've got to be that guy willing to speak up for women and use your power to open doors for them. Janet Petro, deputy director, Kennedy Space Center, reflected that talk isn't enough; you've got to back it up with action:

> You have to take very specific actions to follow up with women and be a deliberate advocate. Don't just say, "Hey, I'm mentoring all these women." You actually have to be accountable to do the things a mentor is supposed to do. Check in with them, meet with them, listen, advocate, create opportunities for them. You have to do this over a long period of time to be credible. Actually make an investment and walk the talk.

Sheryl Sandberg, COO at Facebook and author of *Lean In*, reminds men that creating a more equal world at work, being part of the solution, should be a badge of honor for men, not a source of embarrassment.[20] In our interview with Sheryl, she asserted that we men should mentor women because it's good for us (not just women): "Do it because it's good for you. Don't do it as a favor to women, because if you're the man who more women want to work with, you're going to outperform your peers in the organization. Do it for you, you'll do it better and you'll do it with more conviction."

So *how* can you be "that guy"? Here are some simple strategies. First, lead from the front and set the tone for inclusivity. Too often, men's voices have been absent when it comes to promoting women at work.[21] To be that guy for women, you'll have to work against your natural homosocial behavior and deliberately put women into positions of visibility, giving them both the responsibility and the support to compete for promotions on a level playing field with men. Brigadier General Becky Halstead recalled that one of her mentors, General Hill, promoted her to become his executive assistant. Then, as they traveled around the world visiting other military leaders, he took every opportunity to talk about her and the value added that women bring to the military; he encouraged other leaders to integrate more women into their armed services. Not surprisingly, more women started to pop up in key positions in these countries. It takes a few courageous men to do this first, men who aren't worried what everyone's going to think.

Second, deliberately inquire about the experiences of women in the workplace and then do what you can to address problems and promote equity. At NASA, Janet Petro recalled that her mentor, Robert Lightfoot, did this routinely: "He would ask, 'do you feel that you have been discriminated against on the basis of gender?' I found that so helpful to hear from a male who was truly interested in my experiences and wanted to correct any inequalities. He created a safe space to talk about the obstacles for women. He truly wanted to make sure that neither his own behavior, nor the environment at NASA would get in my way."

Third, deliberately promote formal mentoring programs, especially those targeting women. Then, be among the first to sign on as a mentor. Although most of us prefer mentorships to form naturally, here's the thing: relying on cross-gender mentorships to form organically and informally results in lower rates of mentoring. When mentorships are an expectation, formally arranged and sanctioned, women face fewer barriers to initiating key relationships with more senior men. Laura Behling, dean and vice president at Knox College, recalled being required—as a new assistant professor—to participate in a formal mentoring program: "It forced you to have a mentoring relationship. If there is a formal structure for pairing people so that it is just natural and expected that everyone will have a mentor; that is a key to removing some of the obstacles to having a mentor."

Here is a final strategy for being "that guy": just be yourself. Promoting inclusivity and sponsoring talented women can't be an act. Seriously, guys, women are too smart for that. If you try to sling on your "Super Mentor" cape only when it suits you or when your own boss is watching, you'll be dismissed as a fraud from the start. Coast Guard Academy Superintendent, Rear Admiral Sandra Stosz, framed it this way: "I've seen too many men who put on a persona as the mentor. Women tend to be a lot more collaborative, be themselves more than men do sometimes. So, be yourself if you want to earn a woman's trust."

Will being "that guy" always be easy? At times, men's efforts to champion women are met with suspicion, resistance, even anger—from men *and* women.[22] Your authors' experience as "two dudes" writing a book on mentoring women is illustrative here. When we first began sharing our idea for this book, we got some interesting reactions, everything from raised eyebrows and snorts of laughter to dubious frowns followed by, "but...you're...men..." (as if we'd overlooked that fact). Again, the words of Rear Admiral Stosz: "Sometimes, women are perceived as a risk factor. You have to be a confident man, comfortable in your own skin, willing to take the risk of reaching out to mentor a young woman." Gentlemen, your efforts to promote and champion women in the workplace may meet with initial pushback and derision, even questions about your motives. If this feels too scary or overwhelming, we kindly suggest that you stop whining and grow a pair.

5. Practice Humility (You've Probably Never Been a Woman)

Humility: the quality or state of being humble

Men, don't presume to understand what your female mentee has experienced. It is 100 percent certain that her experiences have been different from yours. Laura Behling, PhD, Dean and Vice President for Academic Affairs, Knox College emphasized the importance of understanding these experiences: "One of the challenges with a male–female mentorship is simply understanding that the women that you're mentoring are not men. They've had different experiences and expectations coming up through the ranks. You don't have to know what those differences are but you do have to be willing to ask about them and then listen."

Few things will get you off to a lousy start more quickly than assuming that your female mentee's life experiences have been just like yours and that you therefore understand exactly where she's come from and precisely where she wants to go. Dana Born, PhD, Air Force Brigadier General (ret), lecturer at Harvard University, explained why male mentors have to be aware of their perceptions: "Recognize that you've not had her experiences. Sometimes, the differences in experience for men and women are significant enough that they've got to be acknowledged upfront and continually as problems arise. Men need to have a sense that women may have had very different experiences in terms of how they're perceived compared to how men have been perceived."

Want some evidence? Here are just a few examples of how women's experiences growing up and entering the world of work have probably differed dramatically from your own:[23]

♦ From her earliest years, she may have been socialized to suppress anger, avoid conflict, and dislike competition, and to think twice about succeeding too much, talking about her accomplishments, surpassing men at work, or asking for what she wants.

♦ In relationships, she's learned to be more comfortable openly expressing her feelings, discussing personal issues, demonstrating affection, and expecting reciprocal (versus hierarchical) relationships with others.

♦ Chances are, she'll experience greater role demands outside of work than you and, therefore, greater tension about how to balance career advancement with family life.

◆ Her definition of career success may be quite different from yours. Perhaps less exclusively about salary, status, and the corporate ladder and more about intrinsically rewarding roles, self-development, and work–life balance.

◆ If she is a woman of color, she may have experienced double jeopardy in her life and career, working against both gender and race stereotypes.

And let's face it: these differences are just the tip of the iceberg. The bottom line is that her journey to this moment in her career has been different from yours. You'll be well served to remember this. Sandra Stosz, Coast Guard Rear Admiral, stressed a female mentee's unique career interests: "So, you're a guy and you want to mentor a woman, learn about where she is and try to meet her there, not where you are. Learn about the woman you want to mentor. Start with 'what are your interests, what are your aspirations and goals, where do you want to go [in your career]?' Meet her where she is and don't presume she's just like you."

These gendered differences in experience can create mentorship challenges for men mentoring women. First, you might have difficulty empathizing with her. If she feels isolated, lonely, and entrapped in stereotyped roles at work, it could be hard for you to "get" her. After all, your experience may be quite different. Second, it may be difficult for her to identify with you if she doesn't see parts of her own experiences embodied in your life and career. And if she can't identify with you, then it may be much tougher for her to use you as a vital role model. Finally, when you discover just how unique and different her life experience and career challenges are, you might feel inadequate to the task of mentoring her. After all, how will you ever be competent enough with the female experience to be helpful? And let's be frank, guys, nothing makes men feel impotent more quickly than not knowing what to *do* and how to *fix* things!

Feeling overwhelmed by the challenge of knowing everything you need to know about women and their distinctive experiences? We have good news for you! *Just be humble.*

If you can check your man ego at the door and approach her with genuine humility, that is, an interpersonal stance that is open and inviting about aspects of her unique experience, then we think the prognosis is good that you *can* be a helpful mentor for women.[24] We are talking here about *gender humility*, the art of being self-aware and humble about what you don't know about women and then being transparent about what you don't know while simultaneously demonstrating honest curiosity about a woman's unique experience and current concerns.

Some men, in an effort to better empathize with their wives during pregnancy, elect to wear a "pregnancy empathy belly" for a period of time to simulate their partner's discomfort and daily experience of pregnancy. In your own way, consider what you might do to approach female mentees with an attitude of humble inquiry about their lives and experiences.

6. She's More Like You Than You Think

News flash from the mentoring front lines: although women have had very different experiences than you, all the evidence shows that they are *not* an alien species! In fact, they're a lot like you when it comes to talents, career aspirations, and dreams about achieving a sustainable work–family life. Here is a simple tip: in most cases, the same things you might share with and do for a male mentee will be just as helpful and appropriate for female mentees (of course, prudence and good judgment are required)!

Guys, we can quickly get ourselves tripped up and tongue-tied when it comes to becoming supportive colleagues for women if we overthink the "gender thing." Yes, it is critical to appreciate her experience as a woman, to approach her with appropriate humility and seek to learn about her unique experiences, both good and bad. Yes, she may have faced more hurdles and obstacles when it comes to credibility and advancement (element 5 made that clear). But if you blow the gender thing out of proportion and behave as though her female status makes her too foreign, alien, and difficult to relate to, we guarantee she'll pick up on your discomfort and insecurity and respond—quite appropriately—by keeping her distance.

Social scientists have clearly documented that gender differences have steadily narrowed since the 1930s. Women and men are more alike in their career aspirations, the jobs they prefer, tolerance for risk taking, probability of assuming leadership roles on teams, assertiveness and dominance, and competence in science, technology, engineering, and math (STEM).[25] Rumors of vast differences between women and men have been wildly overreported. She's way more like you than you might realize.

Sometimes, we hear men use the tired phrase *gender minefield* in their excuses about why they choose not to mentor women: "I'd never get too close to a woman at work, it'd be too risky; I'm sorry, but mentoring women is a gender minefield!" Guys, the only minefield out there is the one women have to navigate when figuring out who the safe and reliable career helpers are. We heard from Brigadier General Becky Halstead on the minefield issue: "There is no gender minefield. Leaders have to do what is right despite the risk. If the standard is not being met, by a male or a female, you as a leader have a responsibility to correct it and not be afraid about a 'gender card' being dropped."

Men, you can change your black-and-white, all-or-nothing thinking about women merely by spending time getting to know a few beyond the superficial hallway hello. We witness this each year at the Naval Academy. Some new male plebes spend their first several months of indoctrination steering clear of female midshipmen, perhaps grumbling under their breath about why a woman would compete for a service academy appointment in the first place. And then, a funny thing happens. As these same young men actually come to know some of their female shipmates, and increasingly come to respect, admire, and appreciate them, they're forced to revise their preconceptions and admit that they enjoy far more in common with women colleagues than they imagined. Mere exposure and friendship go a long way toward melting barriers and highlighting similarities.

7. You Are Neither the First nor Most Important Man in Her Life

For better or worse, we all—women and men—drag our relational histories into here-and-now adult relationships, including our mentorships. Although we like to believe that new relationships—including mentorships—begin tabula rasa, that is, like a blank slate, it turns out this is never the case. This quickly became obvious in our interviews with women; many of them began by describing how their fathers, brothers, and husbands were formative and deeply important mentors. Dr. Susan Madsen, Orin R. Woodbury Professor of Leadership and Ethics at Utah Valley University, recalled that growing up in a home with six brothers made it natural for her to form relationships with men in her career: "I don't worry like some women about relationships with men. It just goes right over my head."

Just as you have man scripts for relating to women forged in the crucible of your own childhood, so too do women enter mentorships with their own scripts for relating to men. One of our favorite John Mayer songs, "Daughters," serves as a reminder to all men that the expectations and reactions of the women we get to know will inevitably be wrapped up in her formative experiences with her father (and to a lesser extent, brothers, boyfriends, or a spouse). Was her father warm, encouraging, and unconditionally supportive? Was he distant, critical, or dismissive of her fledgling ambitions as a girl? No matter what kind of man you are, no matter how benign your intentions, echoes of her father experience will reverberate in your mentorship with a woman. Her previous relationships with men will cast light or shadow on her relationship with you.

Psychologists refer to this process as *transference*: the unconscious redirection of feelings from one person to another. We all tend to repeat in current relationships dynamics from relationships past. Enacting these old scripts often happens below conscious awareness. If you feel disoriented when a mentee is distrustful and suspicious of your motives or reliability, perhaps she is transferring her experience with a cruel sibling or emotionally abusive father. Or perhaps she is overly deferential and compliant, enacting a daughter script from a beloved but overprotective father. At times, a female mentee may unconsciously use a positive male mentor as a *compensatory figure*.[26] This means that, on some level, she is using the mentor to make up for what she didn't receive from her actual parents—often a father. Kathy Hannan, partner, KPMG Inc., underscored the meaning of prior relationships:

> I grew up in a home without a father figure, but did see many men who really cared about girls and young women, be it a

family member, an uncle, teachers in high school, or professors in college. It was really in college that I got the notion that I could build a trusting relationship with someone who cares about me, would challenge me and really get me out of my comfort zone, while at the same time building my confidence.

If you are a solid, caring, trustworthy, and reliable man, there may naturally be elements of your mentoring relationship with a woman that are reparative for her in ways she may only appreciate much later. But here is the catch: you are a mentor, not a psychotherapist. If her relationship with you serves in part to restore her faith in herself and allows her to become more trusting of men, we think that is a wonderful mentoring outcome. But beware the temptation to rescue, re-parent, or heal wounds left by other men. Too many of us can easily get our knight-in-shining-armor or Father-knows-best scripts triggered by a woman who appears injured and vulnerable. Be a steady, unconditional friend and career advocate. Don't become enmeshed in old scripts—rescuer, healer, protective father—that may ultimately sabotage her growth and autonomy.

Gentlemen, remember that her scripts for relationships with guys will often operate below her everyday awareness. It is not appropriate to pry or push her to disclose about her childhood or relationships with other men. Don't be a creep, and watch those boundaries! However, if you notice that her consistent reactions to you appear unwarranted or out of left field (e.g., prickly anger, doubtful suspicion, anxious avoidance), sometimes a simple Socratic question might help set the stage for a fruitful discussion. For instance: "I can't help but notice that you often _____. Can you help me understand what I might be doing to cause that reaction?"

Finally, guys, remember that transference is just as likely to be positive and facilitate a strong mentorship with a woman! Betsy Myers, advisor to Presidents Clinton and Obama, offered an excellent example:

> I would say my dad was someone who always mentored me in a way that taught me about risk taking. He was the one who told me, "Why not try it and go for it." When I couldn't decide about the Obama campaign, he's the one I called and he asked

me, "Why not?" He's the one who taught me to do what you say you're going to do and go for it, work hard, your word is everything, read and study everything to learn your craft, be the best you can, get up early, show up early, those kinds of things.

Retired Air Force Brigadier General Dana Born demonstrated the implications of having a father as a mentor:

When I was sixteen, my mother left the family and my father somehow balanced all of his professional demands with the challenge of raising and mentoring three teenagers. My dad sacrificed tremendously to invest in us, and was the most remarkable mentor and father we could have hoped for. Given this experience, continuing to be mentored by men during my military career felt quite natural.

8. Take Initiative and Be All In

One of the most consistent themes from our interviews with key women in leadership was the importance of having men initiate mentoring relationships. Rather than stand on the sidelines waiting for women to approach them for help, excellent mentors were described as "all in" from the start. They offered career support, advice, and encouragement without being asked. When describing her primary mentor, Admiral Michelle Howard said, "First, he reached out to me, I did not approach him." Betsy Myers recalled that her male career champions were proactive and perceptive: "The beauty of it is they see something in you that maybe you don't see in yourself…they made time for me, made time for meetings, made time to help me deal with whatever was on my mind." These experiences dovetail perfectly with the research evidence. For example, a large study of MBA graduates revealed that when a male mentor initiates a mentoring relationship with a woman, that initial interest and commitment translates into significant and enduring career outcomes; she receives more consistent and higher-impact mentoring.[27]

Guys, we know what you're thinking: Why can't women take the initiative for a mentorship? The truth is that many women do seek career help from men, but they sometimes face resistance and risk career consequences when they try. Because they are frequently excluded from interactions with in-group leaders and key information networks, they have fewer opportunities to be noticed by and naturally interact with power holders, often men.[28] Even if women are noticed, some guys are reluctant to mentor women because they think it's the organization's senior women who should do that. Other men are honestly afraid that they'll say or do something that will get them keelhauled by HR. This means that when a woman approaches a prospective male mentor, it can be like making an unwelcome cold call. In *Lean In*, Sheryl Sandberg commented on this dilemma for women: "Women have been trained to go out and 'find a mentor' in order to make it in their careers. But asking someone to be a mentor can be a total mood killer when it comes to a budding relationship with a senior person…especially when you hardly know the person."[29] Instead, men have got to be intentional about identifying promising women and then reaching out and inviting interaction.

There are other forces keeping women on the sidelines when it comes to seeking out men who might mentor them. Socialization practices can play a role. Sometimes the behaviors girls learn to enact—deferring, taking a passive approach early in relationships—work at cross purposes with attracting a mentor.[30] Guys learn growing up that "fortune favors the bold" when it comes to mentoring—women, not so much. And let's not forget that women take other risks when initiating interactions with men. Again, Sheryl Sandberg pinpoints the concern succinctly: "A senior man and a junior man at a bar is seen as mentoring. A senior man and a junior woman at a bar can also be mentoring…but it looks like dating. This interpretation holds women back and creates a double bind. If women try to cultivate a close relationship with a male sponsor, they risk being the target of workplace gossip."[31]

Gentlemen, are you really all in? Are you ready to be *that guy*? If so, now is the time to step up to the plate and start deliberately interacting with some of those everyday Athenas. What builds good working relationships early on? Quite simply, it comes down to frequency of interaction. In study after study, the *mere exposure effect* in social psychology shows that humans are hardwired to feel attachment and positive feelings for those we see and interact with most often. That means you've got to get out of your office and actively initiate conversations with junior women. Even introverts can do this well; they just have to work harder at it! It won't do to be like one of our favorite undergraduate professors who placed a doormat outside his office that read: *Is this visit really necessary?* And guys, deliberately initiating relationships with women and pushing them into the organizational spotlight will be good for you, too. A recent study from the University of Colorado found that when male executives promoted diversity in hiring and advancement, they got a noticeable bump in their performance reviews. What happened when women pushed for other women? Their performance reviews actually declined.[32]

Gentlemen, we close with a warning about a sensitive topic: the *M word*. We want you to start noticing, initiating conversations with, encouraging, and promoting the everyday Athenas in your workplace. We want you to show that you're all in. But DO NOT call yourself her "mentor." Let her do that. This might seem a bit counterintuitive in a book about mentoring, but imposing a mentor–mentee label on the relationship is presumptuous and may even imply ownership and hierarchy in a way that makes her feel trapped and obligated. Words matter. The term mentor must be earned; it can never be claimed. Later, perhaps much later in her career, she may look back on your efforts with appreciation. She may honor you by referring to you as a mentor. Savor those moments!

7

Matters of Relationship

In this chapter we present a dozen elements that are crucial to forming and cultivating healthy and effective developmental relationships with women. Excellent mentors demonstrate empathy, affirmation, and unconditional positive regard. They are aware of the importance of friendship, openness, and reciprocity in relationships with the women they mentor. And they never ignore the realities of outside perceptions or the challenge created by feelings of intimacy. Finally, effective mentors are self-aware and proactive when it comes to recognizing relationship transitions and endings. Gentlemen, aspire to practice each of the elements in this chapter and you will not only create high-quality mentorships with some of the rising Athenas around you, you will also help your mentees to create mental maps or schemas for what good mentoring looks like. If this kind of mentoring relationship is not the norm in your organization, you can be that guy who sets the standard and starts to create a culture of mentoring that makes other organizations envious.

9. Listen! (Don't Talk So Much)

One of our favorite short videos is titled, "It's Not About the Nail."[1] We use the video when we teach about gender styles in communication. In the video, a woman is sitting on a couch with a man, a look of pained bewilderment on her face. She says, "It's just, there's all this pressure, you know? And...I can feel it, I mean literally feel it in my head. And...it's relentless. I don't know if it's going to stop. That's what scares me the most, I don't know if it's ever going to stop!" Then the camera pans up to reveal a large nail stuck in her forehead. Now the man—perhaps a boyfriend or spouse—points at her head and says, "Well...you do have a nail in your head...I bet if we got that out of there..." Exasperated, she cuts him off and declares, "It's *not* about the nail! Stop trying to fix it!" It turns out that she simply wants him to listen to her.

Although it plays on some gender stereotypes, this short comedic film makes us laugh precisely because it reveals a commonly occurring difference between women and men. Far too frequently, as guys we approach relationships the way we approach a weekend DIY project: identify the problem quickly, grab some tools, and get to work. If you are like many men, you have an extra-large gene for "fixing" problems—and fast. After hearing only a cursory description of another person's concern or dilemma, we leap into action with suggestions, strategies, and solutions. But here is the problem: your mentee may not need or want you to "fix" things for her at work. And frankly, if you try to solve all her problems, you may unintentionally undermine her ability to do it herself. Before you think about problem solving, *first, just listen to her*! When communicating concerns, women often value being heard and understood as much as they value finding a solution.

Gentlemen, remember this: women are often socialized to value connection, commitment, and friendly affiliation in relationships.[2] Studies of women in mentorships reveal that they develop trust in a mentor through the medium of communication and mutual understanding.[3] A mentor who listens, understands, and affirms a woman's unique experiences will be a mentor she can more easily trust and learn to count on. Early in her academic career, Dr. Laura Behling described her mentor's commitment to really hearing her: "Right when I first got to know him, we had a meeting and he sat me down and said, tell me where you want to go. Then, he just listened while I did the talking. That conversation started putting ideas in his head. He started looking for specific opportunities that would help me along my path." If there is one thing we guys need to practice, it's the art of keeping our mouths shut and our ears open. This is especially true early in the relationship when a mentee shares insecurities or questions whether she belongs.

The art of listening begins with sensitivity to the environment. Can you turn away from your computer screen, put the phone on mute, and minimize interruptions? If your office is a hive of activity, perhaps a nearby coffee shop is a better place to talk. Next, think about your nonverbal cues. Are you making good eye contact? Is your posture open (no crossed arms)? When she speaks, can you keep quiet while nodding and using encouraging facial expressions? Finally, can you demonstrate genuine *empathy*? Empathy is the accurate understanding and the ability to react emotionally to the mentee's awareness of her own experience.[4] You need to listen and accurately understand her feelings and concerns. Then you must reflect them back to her without allowing your "fix-it" gene to get in the way. If you can listen and then communicate accurate understanding of what she has to say in an affirming manner, you will be a mentor who builds trust and earns the right to collaborate with her on a way forward.

As the video we described reveals, sometimes, it's not about the nail. Just listen.

10. Let Her Decide (Don't Assume)

She's a woman, therefore she must want _____; she must be planning to _____, and she probably has no interest in _____. Take this sentence completion test honestly. It just might alert you to some of the automatic assumptions you tend to make about women. But gender-based assumptions are often risky. Many of the women we interviewed cautioned men not to assume that women will either want to suspend their careers at some point to focus on starting a family or that women will focus on their careers to the exclusion of all else.

Gentlemen, you may have heard this aphorism: Assuming makes an *ass* out of you and me. Nowhere is this truer than in your relationships with women at work. Even when your assumptions about women are seemingly benign and well intended, they can scuttle her advancement and leave her feeling stereotyped, undermined, and powerless. On this topic, perhaps nobody we spoke with as we prepared to write this book framed the risk more clearly and thoughtfully than Janet Petro's mentor at NASA, Robert Lightfoot:

> I was really fortunate early in my career to have a "tipping point" experience in this area. I was on a selection committee. One of

the other members of the committee was one of my own mentors, a woman. Very quickly the committee reached consensus
on a selectee. As we went around the table to discuss her, I made
the comment: "This job requires a lot of travel and she just had
a baby; I don't know, this would be really tough for her if she
was hired." Fortunately, my mentor looked across the table at
me and said very clearly: "That's not your decision to make! She
knows she has to travel, she knows she just had a baby, don't you
make the job decision for her." That hit me like a ton of bricks.

Even now, after all these years, Lightfoot can still find himself making
assumptions about what women want or what's "best" for them. Unfortunately, even when well-intended, our gendered assumptions about
how best to support female mentees may create disparities and disadvantages. Again, Robert Lightfoot explained:

I still struggle to get this right. For instance, I have a very senior
woman working with me now and she has a couple of teenagers.
I find that in an effort to be sensitive and accommodating to her
work–family demands, I can say something like, "Oh, you don't
have to be at that meeting, it's not important for you to drive all
the way in just for that if you have a family function." But you
know what, her husband is also a senior person at NASA and I
never even think of saying something like that to him.

Here is the rub: we would all appreciate a mentor like Robert Lightfoot. Clearly, he shows empathy for his mentee's work–life demands;
obviously, he has her back in doing what *he thinks* is best for her. He is
willing to provide top cover if she has a family event going on. But, as
Lightfoot himself reflects, even benign assumptions can result in her
subtle exclusion from key meetings. Dismissing her on the basis of gender might just communicate to her and others at work that she's not
an essential and valued team member, at least not in comparison to
her male colleagues. Worst of all, when men make assumptions for a
woman, they undermine her capacity to decide for herself what's best.
Air Force Brigadier General (ret) Dana Born echoed this sentiment:

If you enter a mentorship with a fixed mindset—related to gender or the concerns she might have—you are essentially labeling and limiting your mentee versus fostering a learning orientation in which you try to learn and understand how the mentee sees herself, what she thinks her strengths and weaknesses are, and what matters most to her. Sometimes men assume—you're female so therefore you're going to have work–life balance issues, you'll be pregnant, etc. . . . and that simply might not be the case.

So, guys, here is the bottom line: to the very best of your ability, don't assume, and let her make the call about what's best for her at work and where she wants to go in her career. To do this, you should start by rereading element 9: shut your yapper and just listen. You've never walked a mile in her shoes. So before you assume what she'll need or want to thrive in her career, take the time to learn about her. Listen first. Then, make a habit of checking with her when a decision point arises. For example, you might consider saying, "A slot on a key committee has just opened up. In light of your talent and long-term plans, I thought of you right away. I believe you'd be a terrific addition, and it is a high-profile committee. It does require some late afternoon meetings and I know that would get you home later two days a week. What do you think? I'd be delighted to nominate you if you think the time is right."

Watch your assumptions, discuss things collaboratively, and then, let her decide.

11. Maintain a Learning Orientation

So far so good: you're listening and not talking so much, and you're avoiding quick assumptions about her. Now be sure to keep an open mind and take the time to really learn *about* her and *from* her as the relationship progresses. To understand what you need to know *about* her, you'll have to be welcoming, invitational, and available. You'll have to initiate meetings and conversations and stay tuned to her experiences, aspirations, and concerns. As you patiently observe and listen, you'll discover what her priorities related to work–life balance look like. As trust develops, you'll catch glimmers of her unique career dream. Then you can collaborate with her in developing a strategy to get there.

But just as important as learning *about* her, you've got to be open to learning *from* her. If research evidence in the field of mentoring confirms one thing, it's that excellent mentors honor and respect the contributions of the mentee.[5] Having a mentor who is open and collaborative is deeply meaningful and particularly poignant to people who have been marginalized—in society and in organizations—on the basis of gender or race. Your mentorship with a woman can help her learn about male behavior and attitudes, especially those linked to success in the organization. But just as important, she can teach you about feminine decision making, communication, and leadership styles. In an open and trusting relationship, you'll hear about her unique experiences as a woman; these are bound to be eye opening. Learning about these things from a female mentee and then communicating genuine appreciation for her contribution to your own development as a person and a leader will be an incredibly powerful mentoring tool. In you, she will discover a role model who values collaboration, respects diverse perspectives, and affirms her as a colleague with something valuable to offer.

Belle Rose Ragins, an industrial–organizational psychologist at the University of Wisconsin–Milwaukee and a luminary in the mentoring field, has discovered that mutual learning is a hallmark of high-quality mentorships.[6] Her research shows that mentorships that produce the most growth—in both parties—are those relationships that are most reciprocal and mutual. In reciprocal relationships, there is fluid expertise between members. Although mentors, by definition, have more experience in the profession, Ragins concludes that mentees "bring their own insights, life experiences, and talents to the table, and mentors in high-quality relationships value and are influenced by their mentee's perspectives."[7]

Gentlemen, remember this. The best mentorships are reciprocal and collaborative. Wise mentors recognize that expertise in any mentorship shifts depending on the phase of the relationship and the specific issue at hand. Chances are you'll become better at your job, better as a mentor, and better as a man if you are open to learning from her.

12. Be Her Friend

Women often report isolation at work, especially in male-dominated professions and organizations. Many of the women we interviewed told us that when an admired man at work simply offered friendship and support, they felt anchored and empowered to hang in there. When Sandy Stosz became the first woman to take command of a U.S. Coast Guard cutter, she was truly on her own. Living under a microscope, without a single female peer to turn to, she recalled that every order was scrutinized and each decision second-guessed. Her most powerful mentor during that difficult command tour was Dave Foley, an enlisted chief, a guy who really understands that sometimes, all you have to do is "be her friend." Foley recalled that in those days, "She was over at the house often. We'd have cookouts. Sandy got to know my kids. It gave her some release and let her know that people will look out for you when you do a good job as a leader."

Other women provided similar reflections. Susan Chambers, now vice president at Walmart, recalled: "The biggest challenge I had was feeling completely isolated. I just felt really alone. If I took it home, I got my husband upset, which wasn't useful because there wasn't anything he could do about it. There was one other woman, we'd laugh and cry together. She was the closest thing I had to a peer. It's feeling like you have nowhere to take your issues and concerns."

Laura Behling, dean and vice president at Knox College, recalled a male mentor early in her academic leadership career who took the time to check in with her often during a personally trying time: "That gesture, and his recognition that some professional issues were also personal for me and hitting close to home, meant a lot to me. That he, as president of the institution, would take time out, put aside other pressing business of the day, walk down to *my* office and check in with me really made a significant impact. I thought, okay, this is a guy who's really paying attention." Sometimes, a mentor must emphasize the simple act of friendship.

Guys, here's some food for thought. Compared to men, women's self-concepts are often defined more by relationships. The role shifts and relational losses that occur when a woman changes jobs or enters a new career track can threaten her sense of belonging, self-esteem, and psychological well-being.[8] As a mentor, a first order of business is simply engaging her as a friend. And be aware of the *quality* of friendship you offer. Friendship studies indicate that friendships between women are characterized by mutuality, commitment, self-disclosure, empathy, and intimacy.[9] Not so much with men. We guys tend to center our friendships on specific activities: "Dude, let's hit the golf course, watch a ballgame, or have a couple of beers." And while we're engaging our male friends, we tend to talk less, share less, and focus more on outcomes and achievements than the here-and-now experience of our friendship.[10] Furthermore, gender differences can be heightened in periods of significant stress. Faced with stress, men tend to respond with "fight or flight." Their response to threat may be balling their fists and preparing for combat. In contrast, women who are significantly stressed tend to "tend and befriend." That is, they search for friends, seeking and offering support.[11] Conclusion? If we avoid intimacy and connection in our friendships with women, trust may fail to develop and a potential mentorship might die on the vine.

Gentlemen, there's no razzle-dazzle required here: just be there for her, ask her how she's faring, let her vent to you in confidence, and make sure she's included in social events. At times, the most effective mentor is a reliable friend.

Here's a last lesson: be her friend for the long haul. Even when she's promoted out of your department, changes jobs, or leaves the organization, reach out to her from time to time. Let her know you're still in her corner, still standing by, still a champion for her career and a sounding board when she needs one. Janet Petro recalled that her mentor at NASA, Bill Parsons, took initiative to maintain their friendship for years, long after Bill had departed to become director at the Kennedy Space Center. "Bill was willing to maintain an ongoing collegial friendship and partnership with me over the years," Petro said. "That was key. Then, he called me up one day and asked me to join the team at Kennedy."

Excellent mentors remember their mentees. They stay tuned and available. They reach out to check in from time to time, long after the active phase of the mentorship has ended.

13. Be Honest, Direct, and Unconditionally Accepting

Legendary counseling psychologist Carl Rogers observed that, in order to truly help another person grow, you've got to demonstrate three qualities: *empathy*, *genuineness*, and *unconditional positive regard*.[12] Element 9 was all about empathy. Now, let's talk about being genuine and unconditionally accepting.

To be genuine as a mentor, you've got to be yourself in the relationship; no facades allowed. Freely admit your own imperfections and the limits of your own knowledge and expertise. And genuineness requires something more: you've got to tell your mentee the truth about how she's performing and what she needs to work on. You've got to give her the unvarnished, brass-tacks feedback she needs to sharpen her game and compete. Sometimes, delivering direct and honest correction will be hard for you and painful for her. But look, if she can't count on her mentor to give her straightforward feedback, who *can* she count on?

To a person, the women we interviewed most appreciated men who told them the truth flat out. Susan Chambers, vice president for Walmart, recalled that her mentor demonstrated his firm commitment to her through painstaking honesty—sometimes with brutal directness—in his feedback: "I've never had anybody in my life, save for maybe a parent, who was more intensely interested in making me better. I never doubted that was his primary objective. It was unvarnished. It would be as close to a military experience as I could imagine. He set a very high bar, just as high—no lower and no higher—than for my male counterparts. This allowed me to compete."

Being genuine and direct with feedback sounds easy, right? Hold on, guys, it appears men have a glaring Achilles heel when it comes to giving women constructive feedback. Men often pull punches and sugarcoat reality for fear of "hurting her feelings" or "making her cry." There is evidence that men are inclined to back off and soften their corrective feedback to women, especially when tears or other evidence of emotion enter in. At the Navy's Survival, Evasion, Resistance, and Escape (SERE) School, trainers tell us that during the much-feared prisoner of war experience, male interrogators must be carefully monitored when interrogating women. Not because they become harsh or abusive.

Just the opposite; they tend to ease off at the first sign of genuine distress in a female detainee. Ironically, when a male detainee shows weakness or tears, interrogators often become even more forceful.

You see the problem here. We men appear hardwired to back off when women manifest the first traces of distress or emotion or, God forbid, tears. But if women in SERE training aren't fully inoculated, they'll be more vulnerable and less adaptive later, perhaps in combat or captivity, when lives hang in the balance. Our inclination to protect may be harmful to the very women we're trying to mentor. Several women we spoke with recognized this phenomenon. Rohini Anand, Sodexo senior vice president, said, "Looking back, it's what they [male mentors] didn't do that hindered my success. None of them ever really gave me critical feedback. I see feedback as a gift and I wish I'd had more of it. Female mentors were better at giving me the feedback I needed to improve." Dr. Susan Madsen of the Utah Women & Leadership Project reflected that, far too often, male mentors feel they have to "tiptoe around" for fear of harming or offending a woman: "There's a funny dynamic in many relationships between men and women. Men struggle with 'how much should I say? I don't want to offend; will she go home and cry?' If they tiptoe around then they really can't mentor at the depth that may be most helpful for women."

Now, gentlemen, a word about that other critical element of helping relationships: *unconditional positive regard*. Rogers defined this as the ability to convey a warm acceptance of her experience and a prizing of her as a person, regardless of how she happens to be performing.[13] Yes, we've told you to be direct and honest, but never forget: kindness and honesty are *not* incongruent. To be an excellent mentor for women, you've got to master the art of direct, transparent, and to-the-point feedback, but you've got to deliver it thoughtfully; this is no time for anger or shaming. Again, several of our interviewees including Betsy Myers commented on their mentor's skill at blending feedback with commitment and unconditional regard, "it think it's hard to tell someone 'your dress is getting in the way.' You have to build trust with her and give honest feedback to let them know what they need to do to succeed. When it comes from a place of love and you know someone cares about you enough to ensure you succeed in that organization, then that advice is taken to heart."

Alice Eagly described the supportive and affirming nature of her mentor, "He was very nonjudgmental. There was this implicit understanding from him that everything would work out. So, it was really his supportive nature more than anything I learned from him in a professional sense. After interacting with him, he never made me feel less competent."

As is true in most other interpersonal relationships, a mentorship will be far more effective if your mentee sees evidence that you are there for her in good times and bad. Your mentee will make mistakes, fail to implement your advice now and then, have crises from time to time—both personal and work related—and will otherwise behave imperfectly; in other words, she will behave like a human being. To be effective, be absolutely certain that you refrain from communicating that your support and acceptance are contingent on success, let alone perfection.

Give her the feedback she deserves and needs to be successful. You owe it to her, yourself, and your organization. But never forget to do it in the context of transparent commitment and unconditional acceptance.

14. Affirm That She Belongs (Over and Over Again)

If you only get a few things right when mentoring a woman, be certain that consistent *affirmation* is near the top of the list. If nothing else, remember this: not only do women face more external/organizational barriers to promotion; they face internal, self-sabotaging barriers as well. These include internalized stereotypes, self-doubts, and even shame about wanting to soar in their careers.[14] In male-centric environments, women are more likely to suffer bouts of the *imposter syndrome*, secretly believing they don't belong, that they were hired or promoted by mistake, and that it's only a matter of time before they are revealed as frauds and shown the exit.[15] Trust us on this; you will encounter rising Athenas with sterling records, glowing resumes, and obvious brilliance, yet they may suffer with self-doubt, feeling like imposters. Sheryl Sandberg told us that there is a perfect storm of factors in play here. Not only is the performance of women at work systematically underestimated and undervalued compared to men, women are also likely to feel less confident in *themselves*. In her first job as a research assistant to a chief economist,

Sandberg was plagued by concern for how little experience she had with a critical computer program. In that moment, it was her mentor's steady affirmation and unwavering belief that kept her moving forward.

In male-dominated organizations, one of the culprits causing women to engage in self-doubt is the phenomenon of *stereotype threat*. Experiments show that merely reminding a woman of her gender immediately before she takes a math test—a domain in which we all expect men to perform better—will lead to a measureable reduction in her performance.[16] The same applies to any task or performance domain that gender stereotypes tell us should favor men—including leadership.

So what can you do for your female mentee? With grace and good humor, be sensitive to signs of the imposter syndrome and look for every opportunity to remind her that you believe in her; remind her that she *does* belong and that she *is* competent. Convey often how delighted you are that the organization had the foresight and wisdom to hire her! The excellent mentor expresses unwavering belief in her talent and potential, especially on the days when her own reserves of confidence and esteem are running thin. Never underestimate the power of your own affirmation in convincing her to stay in the fight.

The power of a mentor's affirmation was confirmed in an extensive study of women in the academic faculty pipeline. Etzkowitz and his colleagues discovered that: "Many women offered 'fork-in-the-road' stories in which, having plummeted into depression, confusion, and uncertainty, they sought the counsel of faculty members about whether they should continue. They were prepared to accept their professor's assessment of their ability and performance, so long as this was conveyed in a manner that suggested he or she cared one way or another about their well-being."[17] Expressions of support by these mentors were defining in their decisions to continue.

Finally, gentlemen, be particularly attuned to a female mentee's need for affirmation when she experiences a setback or perceived failure. Nadine Kaslow, past president of the American Psychological Association, observed that "it is very important to be sensitive to emotional reactions that occur in response to real or perceived failures or setbacks. I think that women often take those really hard and it can get in their way." When Brigadier General (ret) Dana Born was dean of the Air

Force Academy, the institution received a very negative Inspector General Investigation report. Born recalled:

"The findings were quite negative and felt devastating. I felt personally responsible as one of the key leaders. The next morning, I delivered my letter of resignation." Her mentor, the Academy Superintendent, was a man who understood the art of deescalating emotional reactions and providing heavy doses of affirmation. "He asked me to sit down, handed me a bunch of tissues and said, 'Listen, you are an excellent representative of this institution. I am not going to accept your resignation. Now, if you're going to join me in the Board of Visitors meeting that starts in a few minutes, why don't you go use my personal restroom, freshen up, and let's press ahead.' He was just so solid. The key was his incredible belief in me and support at a crucial moment."

15. Leave Your Competitive Instincts at the Door

If you're a man, chances are good you were socialized to value authority, competition, and individualism. As little boys, most of us were mesmerized by stories celebrating the *heroic journey*.[18] By now, you know it well. Young man leaves family and friends, goes it alone into the competitive world, and endures a perilous journey before a final triumphant return! If this time-honored narrative of manhood were confined to childhood stories, all might be well. But the truth is that in many male-centric professions, guys continue to prize competitive individualism and a boot camp mentality designed to thin the herd and distinguish manly men from cream puffs. The heroic journey model of mentoring is stoic, hierarchical, and relationally detached. In this model, learning is a one-way street; the wise mentor is the conduit for knowledge and the mentee is a passive learner.

So what's the problem you ask? Simple. The heroic journey approach to mentoring is based exclusively on antiquated visions of male development. It is often entirely incongruent with the characteristics women prize most in relationships. In fact, few things can cause your mentorship with a woman to founder so quickly as being distant, paternalistic, or competitive. Most women are not seeking a *heroic master–apprentice* mentoring relationship. Remember, women have been socialized quite differently. Chances are, your female mentees will value integration over separation and interdependence over heroic independence. They are more likely to seek mentorships built on power sharing, mutuality, equality, cooperative learning, and the integration of personal and professional lives.[19] You really want to be "that guy" who mentors women well? Then you'd better check your urge to outshine them. Let's face it, a confident man no longer needs to remind everyone he's the biggest and best in the room—little boys need that. Although guys often learn early that competition and hierarchy are the building blocks of relationships, the truth is that women rarely feel the same.

So what's the alternative to the traditional competitive, top-down mentorship style? Evidence from decades of research on how women best learn in school and thrive at work shows that they soar in an atmosphere of collaboration. These more collaborative models are called *co-mentoring, professional friendship*, and *power-with relationships* by various authors, and women clearly prefer mentors who are collaborative and power sharing in their approach to mentorship.[20] We prefer the term *transformational mentoring* to describe the kind of relationship most likely to work well with the women you champion at work.[21] Here are some of the key practices of transformational mentors:

- Deliberately partner with your mentee in sharing information and discussing the best way ahead for her.
- Encourage open, mutual conversations that are not defined by rigid expert–nonexpert or master–apprentice roles.
- Communicate concern for both her professional development and her personal growth.
- Resist the urge to flaunt your positional power and comparative experience.
- Be humble; recognize that your vulnerability and authenticity will serve as a good model while strengthening your bond.

Want your mentee to shine? Want your mentorship to work for her? Then, create a relationship defined by openness, sharing, teamwork, and collaboration. Let her victories and advancements be your victories too. And when she begins to surpass you—and you should encourage and expect this—don't sulk. Rather, recognize and celebrate the milestone and express genuine pride in her accomplishments.

16. Be Attuned to Outside Perceptions and Discuss Them Openly

People talk.

Understand that human beings come hardwired to gossip, rumormonger, and pass along the latest titillating scandal. When a man and a woman become engaged in a close developmental relationship at work, eyebrows raise, jealousy blossoms, and idle minds begin to race. As a male—and particularly a male with some power in your organization— you need to accept that everyone is watching.

Mentoring research is quite clear when it comes to the effect of gender on after-work socializing between mentor and mentee. When a man mentors a woman, the two are far less likely to engage in extra-work meetings than pairs of the same gender, for fear of the relationship being misconstrued by others.[22] Two men meeting after hours? No harm, no foul. They're obviously working. But a man and woman? Oh my, it's fifty shades of gossip. When Becky Halstead was selected as General Salomon's aide, she came face to face with outside perceptions: "Are they getting too close? How do they talk to each other? Everyone just watches you." Sadly, fear of external perceptions often results in fewer mentor–mentee interactions, fewer opportunities for her to be mentored.

Here's the thing, gentlemen: no matter how much it may feel like walking on eggshells and no matter how much you resent it, you owe it to her to be sensitive to the way outside perceptions can harm your mentee, possibly even damage her career. The toxic effects of external perceptions come in three primary forms. First, rumors and accusations of sexual involvement may pose a barrier to women in initiating interactions with senior men at work.[23] Even when you are welcoming and supportive, she may avoid you for fear that her efforts will be misconstrued as a sexual advance by someone in the organization. Kathy Hannan was the victim of such workplace innuendo: "Sadly, I was not aware of most of it until after I had moved on, but I did hear about it later. At the time, I recall one woman saying, 'She always gets a meeting with him even when others can't, there's something going on there.'" Kathy Kram discovered, in her pioneering study of mentorships in organizations, that when a senior male takes an interest in the development of a junior female, there are rumors about the nature of the alliance. In same-gender relationships, everyone assumes the mentor perceives the junior as very competent. In cross-gender mentorships, we question whether he might have other motivations.[24]

A second risk to your mentee is the ubiquitous jealous coworker. Susan Chambers recalled that her mentor was harder on her than on anyone else on their team: "My peers took that in different ways. Some felt lucky that it was happening to someone else. But a couple of people were jealous of the attention he was focusing on making me better." Don't ignore the risk to your mentee when jealous coworkers deliberately fabricate rumors about sexual intimacy. Peer resentment is most salient in competitive workplaces with comparatively few women. Rivalries among women may be exacerbated when a solo woman receives special attention and coaching from a senior male.[25]

So what's the risk to your mentee? She may become a lightning rod for resentment and animosity. Sandy Stosz discovered that when her mentor departed the organization, she paid a price: "People are going to resent you for having greater access than they do. You have to watch out for that. After my mentor left, some people turned against me, they felt threatened." Likewise, Rohini Anand found that her mentorship with a senior male made coworkers distrustful and standoffish: "Some people wouldn't trust me, thinking I would go to [my mentor]. Although I never did, I think that was the perception." Finally, resentment-fueled gossip and alienation from peers may discredit her (she's probably sleeping her way to the top, wink, wink).

A final cost to your mentee may occur when one or both of you respond to public scrutiny by withdrawing from the relationship, avoiding one-to-one meetings and interacting less. When this happens, you'll have fewer opportunities to provide career and social support; the quality of the mentorship will undoubtedly suffer.

Is there any antidote to viral rumors and toxic resentment? We have good news, gentlemen. There are several steps you and your mentee can take to both prevent and mitigate gossip. You must start with accepting that you'll always have *two* relationships with the women you mentor. The first is the *actual* relationship; the one that's on the up and up, focused exclusively on her growth and promotion. The second and equally important relationship is the *external* relationship, the one the rest of the organization is watching.[26] Guys, you own some responsibility for what others think about your mentorships with women. Don't try to shirk it. Get out front and deliberately manage the external relationship. When mentoring a woman, your challenge is to protect the integrity and value of the relationship while protecting her from an external relationship that appears suspect. Here are some straightforward steps to take:

◆ *Be transparent*: Be entirely open about the mentoring relationship. Never appear guarded or secretive about your commitment to championing her development. In hypercompetitive organizations with few women, transparency might also be served by conducting meetings in public, and with the door wide open.

◆ *Don't be exclusive*: Offer all of your mentees, men and women, the same time, attention, and access. Janet Petro recommends: "Don't mentor just one woman. Mentor several women (and men); don't be exclusive with only one." Similarly, Deborah Gillis was able to successfully ignore some minor gossip because, "My mentors made mentorship and sponsorship core to who they were as leaders. I was not an anomaly."

◆ *Check yourself*: If rumors arise, first, ask yourself why. Make sure the gossip has no toehold in reality. Are feelings of attraction or a wish for greater intimacy fueling the office whispers? If so, check yourself, talk to a trusted male friend, and take steps to get the relationship back within professional boundaries.

◆ *Discuss your relationship—actual and external—openly with your mentee*: Collaborate with her to keep the relationship as transparent and open in the workplace as possible. Discuss rumors nondefensively, confront them if necessary, and modify your habits of interaction as necessary to avoid needlessly fueling them.

◆ *Discuss your family, with your mentee and everyone else*: If you are
a husband or a father, it can be helpful to talk about your family openly
and often. Doing so can disarm potential misperceptions about you and
your female mentee. It can also serve as the equivalent of a cold shower
should any romantic notions begin to take form in your mentorship.

Believe it or not, gentlemen, there is often a silver lining when the external relationship is scrutinized. The challenge of managing your mentorship transparently and collaboratively can actually bring you closer
together and serve as a catalyst for a discussion of workplace politics that
may serve her well in her career.[27]

17. In Public, Treat Her Like You Treat the Guys

Don't sabotage your mentee by treating her differently than you treat
her male peers. If the mentor accords a female mentee special access,
special privileges, or other atypical displays of accommodation or affection, she may be ostracized, resented, and rumored to be "involved"
with her mentor.

Many of the women we heard from emphasized the importance
of their mentor making no distinction between them and their male
peers—usually the majority—at work. It was important for their credibility and for public perceptions of the external relationship that the
mentor had consistent standards of performance for men and women,
and that he avoided favoritism. Sandy Stosz learned to appreciate her
mentor's scrupulous attention to professionalism and decorum when she
took command of a U.S. Coast Guard cutter. "He went out of his way to
be ultra-professional and never let anything familiar enter in to the relationship," Stosz said. Her mentor, Dave Foley, echoed the importance of
professionalism and consistent standards regardless of gender: "The key
is to hold women to the same standards. If women aren't expected to do
the same things, it undermines their credibility. I would always encourage women not to allow themselves to be taken off difficult assignments
simply because they were women (e.g., going out in especially rough and
dangerous seas)."

Attention to the way you treat men and women applies to every facet of your public behavior. This goes for physical contact, too. Kathy Hannan cautioned, "Don't treat me different from the men. If you slap men on the back or touch them on the shoulder, then it's okay to do that with women, but don't treat women differently." If you only shake hands with men, you should only shake hands with women, otherwise something as ordinarily benign and thoughtful as a pat on the back or a hand on a woman's shoulder may signal to others in the workplace that the relationship is unduly familiar and that she is receiving unfair advantage.

You should also strive for parity in your approach to scheduling and conducting meetings.[28] Schedule meetings in advance and publicly to reduce the appearance of "spontaneity" in your meetings with a female mentee. If the door is typically open when you meet with a male, by all means, keep it open when you meet with her. In *Lean In*, Sheryl Sandberg describes a strategy developed by Bob Steel at Goldman Sachs for ensuring that men and women could feel equally comfortable meeting with him without fear of gossip.[29] His "Breakfast or Lunch Only Policy" eliminated the option of after-hours meetings with the boss, something that might exclude many women.

Treating her like the guys in public even extends to very nuanced social behaviors that many of us might miss if we're not vigilant. For instance, be attuned to using the same language, greetings, and tone of voice with your mentee that you use with other colleagues in the organization. If you tend to employ humor or a bit of teasing with the guys, failing to do the same with your mentee can make her feel like an outsider. It may also be a subtle cue to onlookers that there is something "special" about your relationship. Of course, "special" is the seed from which innuendo and gossip will soon blossom.

18. Let Her Cry If She Needs to Cry

On the whole, women are freer with tears than men. So gentlemen, as a mentor for women, here is your challenge: if and when she cries, don't freak out! Her tears are not a sign of weakness, incompetence, or fragility. Tears are not inconsistent with excellent work, including first-rate leadership. If your female mentee tends to cry more than you do, if tears help her express frustration, anger, or self-doubt, then keep a box of Kleenex handy, be empathic, and don't dare allow a few tears to diminish your regard for her.

A typical scenario might unfold this way: it's Monday morning, and you're sitting in your office. There's a knock at your door. It's your mentee. You wave her in and turn to hit *send* on that e-mail. By the time you turn back, the door is closed, she is seated, and yep, those are tears, all right. At that moment, an excellent mentor does not have the option of tossing a yellow referee flag, blowing a whistle, making a time out gesture, and saying, "Whoa, there! I'm a mentor not a therapist! I don't do tears!" Sound absurd? Believe it or not, we know men who'd be more comfortable being waterboarded than asked to respond calmly and supportively to a woman's tears. Seriously, we're not asking you to conduct ongoing counseling with her. Just be there.

Here's the thing, gentlemen: if you can't tolerate a few tears, you might not be cut out for mentoring. Of course, you also might not be cut out for marriage, parenthood, close friendships, owning a pet, or generally taking part in the human race. Might she cry more often than you? Maybe. But who cares? Take tears in stride. If you find tears upsetting, remember, the only cure for anxiety and discomfort is exposure. So watch reruns of *Oprah* nonstop until the sight of a crying woman no longer fazes you!

19. Welcome Increasing Friendship and Collegiality

The evidence is in. Mentees consistently report feeling affirmed and valued when their mentors are increasingly willing to treat them as colleagues. As your mentee develops and her competence and confidence increase, it will do her good if you welcome and enjoy more friendly and collegial interactions with her. It can be deeply meaningful and profoundly validating for your mentee if—over time—you acknowledge her growth and professional gains by responding to her more and more as you might a peer. When you do this, you are telling her, "You've arrived. Welcome to the club. I'm proud of you!"

Even though your mentorship with a woman may begin in the context of a hierarchical supervisory relationship—maybe you are her manager or teacher—it will be a very powerful mentoring technique if you work to transform her from an apprentice to a colleague. To do this well, you've got to provide consistent social support, demonstrate that you are trustworthy, and find ways to inspire and challenge her. As she becomes more confident about you, and as she sees you willing to give *and* take in the relationship, chances are that you will both enjoy shared interests, creative energy, and a good emotional connection.

Here is a caveat: be cautious not to expect mutuality and collegiality in your mentorships to develop at the same pace. Several variables will enter in here. Certainly, your mentee's background and culture will play a part. Does she come from a culture steeped in hierarchy and authority? Is she particularly deferential and formal? Do you detect that some difficult life experiences—possibly a bad relationship with her father—make it hard for her to trust and open up? Is your organizational context highly traditional or gender segregated? If so, be careful not to press her for friendly collegiality; this could feel destabilizing and disorienting for her. Rather, by your behavior, demeanor, and welcoming style, communicate that you are open to a more friendly relationship. We often find this to be the case in the military when senior men are mentoring junior women—disregarding rank and appropriate decorum can be uncomfortable for the mentee.

Of course, one of the mentoring elements required of you if you are to guide the mentorship in the direction of mutuality is *self-disclosure*. A professional friendship is a two-way street. As any relationship grows, as trust displaces anxiety, we naturally share more and more with one another. We share triumphs, successes, mistakes, and dreams. And remember this: self-disclosure tends to elicit more disclosure from partners. It is reciprocal. So, as she discloses things to you in the relationship, you may feel obliged to respond in kind. As a general rule, women tend to be especially skilled "openers"; that is, they are better than men at eliciting intimate disclosures from others, even guys who don't normally disclose much.[30] For the most part, sharing more with a mentee as time goes by is a good thing. It deepens friendship and solidifies the relationship as an important collegial connection for both of you. But, self-disclosure also deepens intimacy. As you share more and as you grow to respect, admire, and like her, the positive emotions tied up with openness and sharing can lead to feelings of attraction on both sides.[31] Gentlemen, it's on you to keep the relationship developmental and professional, not romantic. The mature man uses increasing trust, friendship, and openness in the relationship to validate that he sees her as a colleague. The wise man respects the power of self-disclosure and emotional connection to fuel feelings of intimacy; he takes care to channel these feelings appropriately.

While continuing to respect boundaries and honor workplace perceptions, deliberately find ways to communicate that you welcome her feedback, trust her judgment, and see her through the lens of an admiring colleague. Such collegiality and friendship serve to endorse and affirm her status as a competent professional in the workplace.

20. Prepare for Transitions and Endings

Change to mentorships is inevitable.

Eventually, your mentee may graduate, receive a promotion, or change offices or organizations. Before she goes, you owe it to her to talk about it. Mindful mentors understand the importance of preparing for necessary transitions in the life of the mentorship. They learn to celebrate mentee transitions and leave taking. It is important to find a way to honor the importance of the relationship and explicitly discuss transitions *as* they unfold. And, by all means, if a genuine ending is near, talk about it *before* it occurs.

Endings are hard. Sometimes they are painful. In any long-term mentorship worth its salt, you will develop some emotional attachment to your mentee and she to you. Too often, guys don't do goodbyes well. In the military, we often see men who have served together in intense deployment situations part ways with a back slap and a "See you around, dude!" This approach is certainly easier but it's not likely to be very satisfying or helpful to the women you mentor. As a mentor, you owe it to your mentee not to allow a meaningful relationship to end suddenly or fade away unrecognized. Chances are that if you have feelings (e.g., sadness, anxiety) at the prospect of losing such an important and enjoyable professional connection, she will too.[32] Take the lead in talking about it. Make the inner world of thought and emotion explicit in a way that brings meaningful closure for both of you.

Guys, none of us like to admit this, but sometimes, when we grow bonded to a woman in our professional lives, we come to depend on her in ways we don't fully grasp until it dawns on us that she no longer "needs" us as much or until the day comes when she shares the exciting news that she's received a promotion or a new job offer; she's leaving. Naturally, we might experience loss and sadness when this happens. But some men get unconscious dependency issues triggered and so—fearing abandonment and loneliness—try to postpone or even undermine a mentee's independence. This is understandable but unacceptable. Remember element 1: do no harm.

In their interviews with 120 women in various professions, Joan Jeruchim and Pat Shapiro discovered that some men have trouble with ending a bonded relationship; many were ill equipped to give words to the loss they were feeling.[33] But for her sake, you must let her go to become her own professional. Other researchers have shed light on the phenomenon of *sticky relationships* between a woman and her male mentor.[34] Evidence shows that when a woman continues to rely exclusively on her early career mentor—versus a rich constellation of helping relationships—for subsequent career support, her self-efficacy is threatened; sticky ties with a mentor may limit her belief in her capacity to successfully manage her own career.

Gentlemen, take heart. There are several specific things you can do to celebrate your mentee's development, independence, and ultimately, her leave taking, in a healthy and affirming way.[35]

♦ *Accept transitions and endings*: Don't pretend the relationship will go on as it is forever. Recognize that her growing independence and career promotions are a nice validation of the success of the mentorship.

♦ *Work on self-awareness*: Ask yourself honestly how you feel about her less frequent interactions with you, about her growing self-confidence and independence. Be aware of the patterns in your history of relationships with women at work. Do you do endings well?

◆ *Narrate both the process and the outcomes*: Be deliberate about discussing upcoming transitions in your relationship. Be honest about your mixed feelings, perhaps pride in her accomplishments and sadness at seeing her go. This will give her permission to do the same. And always highlight how far she has come and your admiration for her.

◆ *Arrange a time to celebrate and say goodbye*: Perhaps a nice lunch or even just a scheduled meeting at a favorite coffee shop will serve as a good venue to reflect on the relationship, express thanks, and say goodbye—at least to the active or working phase of your mentorship. Tell her what you have most admired and appreciated about her and what you'll miss about working together.

Here is a final word on endings, gentlemen: although men tend to tout the inevitability and the heroic virtue of separation and detachment from their mentors, the same is not always true for women.[36] Many women value ongoing, growth-fostering connections with important career guides, even when they have moved on and no longer see their mentors routinely. Admiral Michelle Howard recalled that her mentor periodically checked up on her, long after his retirement from the Navy. His steady career advice, concern, and support over many decades were extremely helpful to her.

8

Matters of Professional Growth

Gentlemen, this chapter includes eleven elements oriented to helping your mentee learn the ropes and prepare for advancement in your profession or organization. Think of these as the *career functions* of excellent mentorship. Outstanding mentors to women *do* a number of things to push them forward, raise their profile, and help ensure their advancement. For instance, they challenge and inoculate women for the hurdles ahead. They provide valuable insider intelligence and are tireless in making sure they have a place at the table. Powerful mentors open doors, nominate mentees for key roles, share social capital, and become "raving fans" for their mentees around the organization. They are unabashed and assertive about using their own position and influence within the organization to address gender disparities and protect a mentee without overprotecting her. Terrific mentors discern mentees' unique approach to leadership, then help them refine and sharpen it. Finally, a great mentor is a deliberate architect of his mentee's network or constellation of career helpers.

21. Make Sure She Gets Included

Remember that sign on your tree fort or clubhouse when you were kids? The one that read, *No Girls Allowed!* Well, as it was when we were little boys, so it—too often—continues to be when men in the workplace gather together. Although most of us are no longer conscious or deliberate about excluding women from key meetings and social events, women continue to find themselves on the outside looking in.

Sometimes, women get excluded simply because men never stop to consider that they might want to take part. When Admiral Sandy Stosz was a junior officer, she discovered that male colleagues never even thought to include her in key social activities: "When the ship was coming into a liberty port, I discovered that the guys on the ship never thought to include me. When, I'd ask, 'Hey guys, what are you planning to do when we hit Rio de Janeiro?' I found that because I was female, they'd assume I'd have no interest in going out with them into port. But, I had no one else to go with."

At other times, guys fail to grasp the importance of gender inclusivity when planning important meetings or social events. Consider the experience of Kathy Hannan, partner at KPMG, when earlier in her career, someone—undoubtedly a guy—decided that a golf tournament would serve as a perfect "team building" experience for the leadership team: "It turned out that the golf club was male only. I had to be escorted around the golf course. In the evening, I missed out on all the fun and interaction because I couldn't be in the cabin where the men were. So, I was on my own. It didn't feel fair at all. I was happy to be part of it, but I wasn't able to enjoy the full experience."

Guys, must we state the obvious? Bars, strip clubs, and sporting events are rarely appropriate contexts for team building, committee meetings, or key organizational discussions. Organizations with a genuine commitment to gender inclusion can't afford to make women choose between outright exclusion or standing on the sideline in venues where men typically bond. Need to bond with other men? No problem. Just do it on your own time; don't combine male-only meetings or venues with key discussions about business. When you do, women—including those you mentor—are left behind.

At all levels in male-dominated organizations, women can find themselves isolated and excluded from key information, the social capital that men take for granted, the intel that can make or break a career.[1] Far too often, that insider, career-critical information gets shared among men in the locker room or the bar. As one woman extolling the virtue of having a male mentor put it in a *Harvard Business Review* interview, "my mentor is my key to the men's room."[2] Even in the sciences, an arena in which teamwork and collaboration are often critical to mission success, women report social exclusion by men; sadly, these women sometimes attribute the cause of their isolation to some inherent deficit in themselves.[3]

Beyond the *where* we tend to congregate outside the workplace as men, is *when* we schedule these events. Too often, team bonding occurs outside typical work hours that can make it difficult, if not impossible, for women to participate, even when they are invited. For women, evening or weekend events can be more challenging to attend due to family commitments. This is an issue for men as well, but we tend to assume men don't have these conflicts, even though we often do. In the busy and hectic schedules of our work lives, it's often challenging to avoid scheduling after-work events—providing advance notice with longer lead times can help people coordinate and create a more inclusive team event. Be vigilant to your mentee's family commitments, and be a voice for scheduling important work events during a time she can participate.

Sometimes, women get excluded from key meetings or time with key men in the organization on the basis of *fear*. Female congressional staffers on Capitol Hill increasingly find themselves banned from after-hours office time with male politicians—the very guys who could be crucial to their advancement—purely because they are women, and, well, it just wouldn't be fair to those congressmen if meeting with an attractive woman caused gossip and a corresponding drop in poll numbers.[4] Such exclusion is not only unfair—clearly, these staffers have earned the right to be there—it is highly discriminatory and probably illegal.

Gentlemen, if you decide to mentor a woman, it is on you to make sure she gets included. One of the first rules of mentoring is this: make her part of the team, make sure she has a nameplate and a voice at the table, and leave no doubt that you intend to have her included in important conversations. Kathy Hannan recalled that her mentor would insist that she get included in lunches or dinners when key clients or organizational leaders came to town. He never failed to use the moment to introduce her and trumpet her achievements. He also made sure her voice was heard at the boardroom table. Hannan recounted an example from one meeting: "I had been sitting around the key leadership table. At times, I would make a comment and it would get a tepid response, maybe some head nodding. Then, two or three people down the line, a male says exactly what I just said and everyone says 'wow' and starts discussing it like it's a new idea. My sponsor would say, 'Wait a minute. Someone tell me how this is any different from what Kathy just said a minute ago.' So, as a mentor, you have to call it out when her voice is excluded, bring attention to it."

Later, when Kathy was only two weeks post birth with her second child, her mentor arranged for her to give a key address at an all-partners meeting in another city. Although she was still exhausted and recovering, he emphasized that this would be a profound career opportunity, a rare moment to be included in the upper echelons of leadership. Kathy remembers, "He asked me the question, 'What do you need to make this work?' I told him that I needed someone to literally carry my bags. Well, he did that for me, so how could I say no?"

Gentlemen, make sure your female mentee gets included in important meetings and events. Don't leave it to chance or count on others to invite her to join in after-work activities, key social events, and career-enhancing meetings and discussions. You are her mentor; it's your job to do it.

22. Teach Her What She Needs to Know (Provide Access to Hidden Politics)

Sophocles said, "The reasonable thing is to learn from those who can teach." So, *can* you teach? *Do* you? Gentlemen, never forget that direct instruction is one of the most salient mentor functions. Research consistently reveals that clear guidance is among the things prospective mentees most desire in a mentor.[5] High-impact mentors are natural educators; they instinctively provide knowledge and refine a mentee's professional skills. The word "education" stems directly from the root word *educere*, literally, to lead forth, to nourish and bring out potential.[6] It is no wonder, then, that the obituaries of highly regarded mentors nearly always refer to the deceased person's facility as a teacher. Effective mentors create frequent teaching moments by giving advice, recounting their own relevant experiences, and providing consultation for the hurdles ahead.[7]

Want to be a great mentor to a woman? Take the time to teach her what she needs to know to thrive in your workplace. Be particularly vigilant for opportunities to provide her with access to critically important information, intel that might otherwise be unavailable to her. Sheryl Sandberg observed that some high-potential women may have difficulty asking for help because they don't want to appear stumped.[8] So don't wait for her to ask for guidance. Think something might be crucial for her to know? Have you identified a knowledge or skill deficit? Get busy teaching and coaching! Janet Petro's mentor went out of his way to teach her to avoid burning bridges and to maintain amicable relationships at work, even with difficult colleagues. Rohini Anand described how her mentor taught her to let her team come up with solutions, even if she already had solved a problem herself.

Belle Ragins reminds men to help women develop *thriving strategies*.[9] Help your mentee turn negative workplace episodes (e.g., ignorance, prejudice, discrimination) into opportunities for enlightenment and learning; excellent mentors use these momentary setbacks as teaching moments, so female mentees will increase their repertoire of effective responses. And keep in mind that good teaching is multimodal. Depending on the mentee, the lesson at hand, and the context, consider using a combination of direct training, personal disclosures of your own struggles and adaptation, stories about others who have gone before, and direct role modeling of key skills. Catalyst CEO Deborah Gillis provides an excellent account of how her board chairman did that for her:

> I'm a first-time CEO and have been in my role for about a year. The chair of my board is Peter Voser, the former chair and CEO of Royal Dutch Shell. As we go through board meetings, he's very good at giving me feedback, advice and says, "Here's a way that you could have handled the situation differently, or here's the appropriate intervention for a CEO to make in this particular circumstance." Although Peter is the chair of the board,

he is giving me advice on more of a peer-to-peer basis. From his perspective as a CEO who has sat where I'm sitting, he'll say, "Here's my feedback in terms of what went well, where you really hit the mark, and where you can continue to develop."

Gentlemen, there is one more component to excellent teaching: find tactful and appropriate ways to give your mentee the inside scoop about the critical history and hidden politics in the organization. When Betsy Myers was offered a key position in the Obama election campaign, her mentor David Gergen cheered her on, but immediately detected a political red flag. In order to avoid alienating herself from many colleagues who would be supporting the Clinton campaign, "he told me, you need to call all of the Clinton folks who are potentially going to be supporting Hillary and explain that you've been offered this key job." Her mentor understood that hearing the news from Betsy directly would head off hard feelings and prevent negative fallout later in her career. In a similar vein, Laura Behling emphasized the crucial significance of getting the insider perspective from her male mentors: "As a junior faculty member, my two mentors provided the history and backstory that existed among people at the institution, the history that everyone who had been there thirty years was familiar with. My mentors didn't offer this history in a critical way, but conveyed exactly what someone who was new should understand. In some cases, the history pointed out minefields to watch out for, in other cases it helped identify potential allies."

Particularly in historically male organizations, women can easily be cut out of "the know." In the Navy, we call this *the gouge*. Students at the Naval Academy trust their upperclass mentors to pass along the gouge, salient tips for surviving, thriving, and avoiding big trouble. If you want to mentor a woman well, don't neglect to pass along the inside scoop. Teach her about the organization's culture, its assumptions, traditions, and taboos. And perhaps most important, tell her who the safe and dangerous actors are. Who are her likely foes, competitors, allies, and neutral parties? Consider the insider knowledge that was given to Kathy Waller, CFO and executive vice president of Coca-Cola Company, by her mentor Jack Stahl: "I remember one of the things Jack Stahl said to me early on, 'You need to be careful in a company like Coca-Cola, which is a relationship-focused company. You never know who you're going to end up working for. Roles change and people change; some of the people who report to you today, you could be reporting to in the future. So absolutely be nice to everybody.' He said, 'I don't care who it is, what they do, it's going to absolutely matter the rest of your career.' He was absolutely right."

Here is a final word: giving the gouge is never an excuse to monger gossip or undermine colleagues. You've got to transmit essential insider information—to include the subtleties of politics and power—without demeaning others in the name of mentoring. Frankly, you've got no business creating unnecessary fissures between your mentee and others at work. Convey the intel that will help her navigate the terrain successfully but after that, let her decide for herself about the personalities and politics around her.

23. Challenge Her! (And Provide the Support to Go with It)

Inoculation: the process of inoculating; especially, the introduction of a pathogen or antigen into a living organism to stimulate the production of antibodies.

Casting an inspiring vision and then challenging her to achieve it is one of the most important elements of mentoring women. If you back off and temper your expectations—because, well, you know, she's a girl—then you're probably failing her, yourself, and your organization. Gentlemen, this may be one of the toughest mentoring elements to get just right, so listen up! Excellent mentors push, dare, and confront mentees. They are persistent in *challenging* mentees to do and experience things they might otherwise neglect or actively avoid.[10] A wise mentor understands the trials and tribulations women will face on the road to success, and he cares enough to help them build immunity—defenses and key skills—for the journey ahead.

This won't be fun or particularly easy. Most human beings— your mentees included—typically avoid the discomfort, distress, even flat-out anxiety that accompany being pushed from their comfort zone and challenged to take on unfamiliar tasks, large audiences, and "impossible" trials. But to mentor a woman well, you must discover the things she naturally avoids—owing to anxiety or something else—and then push her to deliberately expose herself to these tasks and situations. Does she hate to speak up in groups or take credit for her work? Challenge her to do it, over and over again. Does she break eye contact and lower her voice when confronting a colleague's bad behavior? Take the time to practice a different approach with her; then challenge her to go try it again. All of this is designed to immunize her for the leadership challenges ahead. As one of the first women assigned to a U.S. Navy submarine, Lieutenant Tabitha Strobel recounts how her mentors were deliberate about withholding no punches, challenging her exactly the way the male submariners were stressed: "My department head gave me the same chance to stumble as anyone else, he signed me up for really challenging watches, made sure I was getting challenged just like the guys. As women, we're going to make the same mistakes that everyone else makes, but we're here to learn. I think it really helped that my leadership, my Captain, my department head, they gave me the same tough jobs they would anyone else."

Women *and* men at the Naval Academy are daily inoculated against the profound stress, sleep deprivation, and operational intensity that will confront them shortly after they are commissioned at graduation and begin leading Sailors and Marines in combat. Although an outside observer trailing a plebe during a typical day in Annapolis might feel sympathy for the barrage of stressors and demands she faces, please understand the method behind the madness: anything short of pushing her to the very brink of her resources, constantly testing her resilience, would constitute an inexcusable disservice to a future leader. Gentlemen, don't you dare shirk this vital mentoring function: through persistent challenge, inoculate her against the hurdles ahead.

Many of the women we interviewed confirmed the key role a mentor's challenge played in preparing them to succeed at the highest levels as Rear Admiral Sandra Stosz recounted: "When I was the first female commanding officer and he was the battle group commander, he made everything as hard as possible on me to see if I would break under pressure. He went to extreme measures to give me trials and tribulations. He knew that otherwise, people were going to think he was giving me an easy time because I was a woman." Similarly, Kathy Hannan described how her mentor developed her: "He challenged me to accept an opportunity to address all the partners. He reminded me that it was crucial for my career to get the visibility. I was a young partner. I was female. He knew it was anxiety-provoking and out of my comfort zone but he was there alongside me, carrying my bags and giving me the encouragement to go through with it. Right before I went on, I remember he said: 'You're going to nail it!'" For other women, mentors saw unrealized potential. As Susan Chambers detailed: "He set such high standards and expectations; he expected me to move so much faster and to achieve so much more than I ever had before. At the time, I felt it was unfair. But it's only as I look back that I realize I wouldn't be in my current role without it. I wouldn't have been able to get through the difficulties I've been through if I had not had someone who cared and expected that much early in my career."

If challenging a female mentee sounds easy, we can confirm that it's not. Compared to male mentees, women are significantly less likely to report being seriously challenged and pushed to perform, even by the men who call themselves mentors.[11] So why do we as guys instinctively back away when what a woman needs is firm confrontation and challenge? Here are three top reasons:

◆ Thanks to stereotypes about women's capacities, we may simply hold erroneous notions about how much they can take; men tend to underestimate women's ability to tolerate stress and respond to challenge.

◆ Due to male socialization, we may have learned to treat women with kid gloves. Chivalrous childhood mantras, such as "women and children first" and "boys are tough, girls are delicate"—while certainly well-intended—can leave men with genuine aversion to seeing a woman in any distress. Perhaps unconsciously, we fear that women will "break" if pushed too hard. We back away when what she really needs is for us to throw down a challenge and push her to try something that really scares her.

◆ Women are often socialized to underperform so as not to threaten men, and they may use distress signals (e.g., tears) to trigger male protection. And women may simply be less attuned to performance challenges that guys recognize instantly.[12]

Guys, here's the thing: evidence shows that women who persist and thrive in historically male disciplines are women who have been inoculated to thrive in competitive environments. In the sciences, women who persist have had mentors who challenged them to develop a strong sense of self and defenses that neutralize the worst effects of peer hostility and competitive cultures.[13]

Here is the final component of creating successful challenges for mentees: challenge her to do great things, then, provide unwavering *support* to go with it. Dana Born says, of her mentor, "He challenged me to do things I either hadn't considered or didn't feel qualified to do. The key to whatever limited success I've enjoyed was that he believed in me, trusted me, and always provided the support and top cover to go along with it."

Tailor your challenges to each mentee. Pushing everyone at the same rate and in the same way rarely works. The goal is to incrementally stimulate growth with tasks and assignments your mentee has a good chance of successfully completing. Push her, but don't push so hard that she doesn't succeed and the confidence you have been working to bolster is undermined.[14] Expose her to her fears persistently but gradually.

As a mentor, discern how she'll need to be armed to win the battles ahead. Then, help her polish the skills and develop the armor she'll require. Persuade her of her capabilities; challenge her to perform to that potential; then, applaud each little victory along the way.

24. Walk the Razor's Edge Between Protection and Empowerment

Here is an inescapable truth: on her path to career success, a woman will often encounter political agendas, petty animosities, and abuses of power. The competent mentor must master the art of shepherding mentees through moments of danger and vulnerability. In many contexts, women more than men will encounter mean-spirited criticism, misogynistic male coworkers, harassment—both overt and subtle—dismissive assignments, and tasks likely to sabotage their career trajectory.[15]

Gentlemen, sometimes a mentor must intervene. *Protection* is sometimes required to shield a mentee from unfair, vindictive, or sexist policies or behavior in the workplace. In other words, you may need to signal a willingness to kick a little ass (figuratively speaking) to repel unfair attacks and deter future nonsense. Protection can take a variety of forms, including vocal advocacy in public forums, direct confrontation of hostile actors, slicing through bureaucratic red tape designed to keep her sidelined, and questioning of job assignments unlikely to get her noticed and promoted. And don't think you've got to be a major power broker in the organization to serve as an effective defender for your mentee. When Rear Admiral Sandy Stosz was a lieutenant in the Coast Guard and the first woman to skipper a Coast Guard cutter, her chief boatswain's mate—an older, experienced seaman, an enlisted man, and her subordinate—proved to be a powerful mentor to her, in part because he was a tireless protector behind the scenes. Chief boatswain's mate Dave Foley related his interactions with other men:

> I'd go walking off the ship and there would be some Chiefs sitting around talking her down. I'd tell them, you guys don't know what you're talking about. She's a good officer and this is not a fad [gender integration]. You need to get used to it or get out of the service. Then, of course, the next thing from them was, "so what, are you sleeping with her?" ... We also had a Captain in charge of the area at that time who didn't believe women had any place in the Coast Guard. He kept expressing doubts about Sandy behind her back. I finally just told him flat out, "You know, Captain, the truth is she's very capable. She's smart and she knows what she's doing. You need to back off, give her the leeway to do her job."

Sandra Stosz explained what she learned from Dave Foley's actions:

> For a while the Captain was going to extreme measures to give me trials and tribulations as the first woman CO. Then, finally, one day things started to get better. I was interacting with the Captain one day and he said, "I've backed off you because your Chief boatswain's mate walked in here one day, closed the door, and said, 'Stop picking on our Commanding Officer. It's unfair, it's not right, and we're sick of it onboard the ship.'" By standing up for me to a Captain, he taught me you can stand up to someone much more senior in paygrade if you are right.

Alright, guys, so we've established that you *do* have to protect her at times. But before you go all mixed-martial-arts cage fighter on anyone who gives your mentee a hard time, take a deep breath, and think carefully about how protection can quickly become *over*protection. Effective mentors are firm and clear in confronting injustice but they are simultaneously calm, measured, and diplomatic. If you turn Raging Bull when someone "messes" with your female mentee, we predict that you will lose credibility and undermine her. By appearing too ego involved and arrogantly reactive, you diminish your capacity to be an effective advocate for her in the organization. Worse, such behavior may raise questions about your enmeshment or inappropriate involvement with her. I mean, why else would you behave like a jealous boyfriend?

We appreciate that knowing when and how much to protect is a delicate balance. The tension is inherent in the very term *protégé*, which comes from the French verb "to protect." It is sometimes translated as "a protected woman." A protégé is a person under the patronage, protection, or care of someone older or more powerful. In the original study of cross-gender mentorships at work, Kathy Kram discovered that young female managers frequently found it difficult to achieve autonomy and independence from male mentors because these men became overprotective and smothering.[16] Women can feel fathered to death and paradoxically disempowered if men undermine their sense of autonomy and power. Rather than go charging in when she's struggling with discrimination, harassment, or conflict, consult with her first. Be collaborative, not presumptuous or impulsive. Discuss alternative approaches, empower her to take appropriate action, cheer her assertiveness, and encourage her to role-play difficult conversations with you. Conserve your political capital and directly intervene to protect her only when the circumstances are egregious or the two of you agree this is both necessary and unlikely to undermine her own efforts to assertively address the problem.

Here is a final tip, gentlemen: if you are constantly intervening on behalf of a mentee, perhaps you should soberly consider whether you are turning a blind eye to real problems with her performance. Is she needlessly provoking conflict? Is she performing poorly? Sometimes we can develop tunnel vision with a mentee we really like. But it won't do to ignore evidence of unprofessionalism or subpar performance in women we mentor.

25. Open Doors and Put Her Name Forward

Want to mentor a woman well? You've got to deliberately and proactively open doors and promote her publicly. A recent assessment of women in organizations reveals that high-potential women are over-mentored and under-sponsored relative to their male peers; as a result, they are not advancing at the same rate as men in many organizations.[17] Here's the problem: mentors to women seem comfortable giving them feedback and advice, even care and support, but mentors appear less willing to use their own power and influence to advocate for their female mentees. Guys, sponsor your mentee by trumpeting her successes and promoting her visibility—particularly to key stakeholders—at work. Sheryl Sandberg illustrated how her mentor did this for her:

> When I got to the World Bank, every time Larry Summers introduced me to anyone, he would say, "This is Sheryl Sandberg, she's my research assistant. She was first in the Harvard Economics Department." I told him that was really embarrassing and asked him to stop saying that. He told me, "I'm not going to stop saying it. I know you would never say that about yourself, and I know you're embarrassed, but it's really important that people know that

you're good because they're going to want to work with you more and treat you more seriously. So, even though you're uncomfortable, I'm going to keep saying it." Looking back, he was sponsoring me.

Outstanding mentors draw attention to their mentees by highlighting their contributions and achievements both laterally (to peers and colleagues) and vertically (to superiors).[18] Look for high-profile committees and projects to sponsor her for. Introduce her to power brokers and use the opportunity to mention her accomplishments and credentials. In addition to nominating her widely for key assignments, invite her to collaborate with you on projects so she can share the credit for successful outcomes and get noticed as a rising star. Like Sheryl Sandberg, many of the women we interviewed expressed gratitude for their mentors' proactive sponsorship:

> He opened doors and gave me incredible opportunities as a junior person. For instance, he put me on the editorial board of a journal he edited. When we had meetings of the consulting editors, even though I was the most junior person in the room, he asked my advice publicly. He did this in front of much more senior consulting editors.
>
> —Nadine Kaslow

> He started talking to other people about what I could do. Then he gave me an opportunity to cochair a committee with him that was a faculty committee to set the whole strategic plan on research and scholarship for the institution. It was a high-profile committee and it raised my own profile in the institution.
>
> —Susan Madsen

> He made lots of introductions for me at senior levels at the [Kennedy Space] Center. As an outsider, this gave me instant credibility. He was very inclusive, brought me into senior meetings so I could see how business was conducted. His willingness to make me a part of all of those insider meetings from the start was really key to my success.
>
> —Janet Petro

Give your mentee opportunities to demonstrate her competence, and then go tell key people about it. The goal is to make her increasingly visible in positive ways. Never forget that mere exposure to and familiarity with your mentee will make key leaders more inclined to tap her for choice assignments and promotions. Be her advisor and confidant, but don't stop there: you've got to intentionally market her in the organization and the profession. Finally, be careful not to sabotage her by overpromising what she can deliver or promoting her for tasks prematurely.

26. Share Power and Social Capital

Here is a simple truth: in many organizations, particularly those that are currently or recently male dominated, men have a wider base of power and access to more resources. As a man, remember that sharing your own power with mentees can work wonders at leveling the playing field for women. Studies of women with male mentors show that a mentor's "stamp of approval" leads to increased acceptance and stature among a woman's male colleagues, significantly higher salaries, greater access to important people, and stronger perceptions of legitimacy, by both mentees themselves and others in the organization.[19]

Here's how power sharing works: as you publicly support a woman at work, endorsing her for projects and assignments, putting her name forward often, perhaps even sending her as your emissary to key meetings or events, others in the organization will naturally grant her *reflective power*— power of the mentor by extension. Your sponsorship implicitly communicates this message: *she enjoys my backing, support, and endorsement.* This is powerful stuff. Think of the power and reputation you have accrued during your career as a shield bearing your coat of arms. When you mentor a woman, your coat of arms goes before her to melt barriers, open doors, and provide access to influential people who might ordinarily not give her the time of day.[20] When Janet Petro was recruited by her mentor at the Kennedy Space Center, he used his accrued power to cut through the center's resistance to outsiders and endorse her leadership: "As the center director, he gave me the reins from the start. He said, 'I want you to run the center for me. I'll step back and let you do it. I'll just provide you with support.' He made that very clear to the rest of the senior management team."

One slice of deliberate power sharing involves weaving your mentee into your own web of contacts and relationships; power isn't just who you *are* but who you *know*. We are talking here about *social capital,* the collective value of all your social networks. Why is this so important for your mentee? Our networks of colleagues and associates constitute an informal society in which members are inclined to do things for one another. Think of several of your best buddies and colleagues at work. If one of them asked you for a favor, perhaps an introduction or even a job for one of their mentees, wouldn't you be inclined to say yes? Evidence suggests that you would. Norms of reciprocity in our social networks make us inclined to help one another. Any friend of a good colleague is automatically a friend of mine. So each time you introduce your mentee to members of your own network, each time you invite her to a conference or key meeting and then make sure people hear her name and how terrific she is, you are depositing some of your social capital in her credibility account, thereby helping to fund her future success.

Here is one poignant example of this phenomenon. A study by Harriet Zuckerman of U.S. Nobel laureates revealed that more than half had worked under the supervision and mentorship of previous Nobel laureates. Although comparatively fewer women have become Nobel laureates, these award-winning women are twice as likely as men to have been mentored by Nobel laureates.[21] It turns out that social capital can lead to *social heredity*; in sharing our power, prestige, and resources with junior members of our profession, we pass on a legacy of sorts, helping to enhance the prospects for success of those we sponsor. Like many of our interviewees, Deborah Gillis explained how her mentors provided access to their networks and social capital:

> Chris Brett, a mentor and very successful lawyer, through his influence and relationships, introduced me to the then-leader of the Liberal Party of Canada, Michael Ignatieff, who nominated me to be a candidate for election for Parliament in Canada. Michael did not know me, but the fact that I had a highly placed sponsor who really went out on a limb to introduce me and advocate for me made that possible. When I look back on my career, at every stage and transition there was someone who

opened up a door and advocated for me for that next step or opportunity.

Gentlemen, remember to actively and transparently share power with your mentees. When you sponsor a woman, don't withhold access to key members of your social network, and make certain that you accord her the access, public support, and resourcing she needs to get noticed and get things done.

27. Brag About Her in Public; Provide Correction in Private

Gentlemen, as a mentor for women, here is your mantra: *Praise her in public, correct her in private.*

We've established that women have a tougher time of it at work. When breaking barriers and rising through the ranks, they often live life in a fishbowl and under a microscope. They'll be accorded less latitude for mistakes and failures, and often, they'll feel alone in leadership roles. In you, they'll need a persistent and vocal cheerleader. But their success will simultaneously hinge on your willingness to provide honest feedback and corrective advice.

First, let's talk about bragging on her. To a person, the women we interviewed described their mentors as public cheerleaders and vocal fans. They created opportunities to publicly highlight their mentees' accomplishments, often when the boss was listening. Listen to what this sounds like from several of the women we interviewed:

> David Gergen was my mentor at the Center for Public Leadership. He was always what I call a *raving fan* about me. That's one of the things I've discovered; good mentors are raving fans. They stick up for me, they tell people about my work, and they champion me to other people. David Gergen was always willing to say, "Betsy is terrific! I couldn't do this without her!"
>
> —Betsy Myers

People don't like it when women share their own accomplishments, and men automatically get credit for their accomplishments more often than women do. So women have to have some way for their accomplishments to be known. It is very effective when other people share our accomplishments.

—Sheryl Sandberg

These relationships were based on my mentors' confidence in what I had done and that I could deliver in the future. They believed that I deserved those opportunities. Richie Mann would describe how I performed and reacted during times of organizational stress, he talked about how I remained focused on getting the job done, delivering the results and keeping people aligned. He saw something in me early on and acted on that.

—Deborah Gillis

Elements 25 and 26 urged you to open doors, put your mentee's name forward, and transparently sponsor her by sharing power and social capital. That is all well and good, but while you're at it, feel free to crow about her talents and achievements. It is good to play the part of proud mentor. If, in the words of Betsy Myers, you can become a "raving fan" for her, chances are others in the organization will take note of her work. Just as important, your mentee will feel buoyed and heartened. Her own self-confidence and self-perception as a capable, competent rising star will be bolstered. And when the going gets tough and self-doubt creeps in—and it will—she can borrow from your reserves of confidence in her.

At the same time, gentlemen, never withhold correction. When your mentees get it wrong or make a blunder, be direct and honest in letting them know precisely how they've erred and share strategies to correct the problem. Because no one is perfect, your mentees need you to provide constructive criticism designed to rectify shortcomings and help them amend their approach. If not you, the guy who's committed to champion her, then who? In our conversation with Sheryl Sandberg, she shared how she blundered in a big way when helping her mentor, Larry Summers, then chief economist for the World Bank, prepare for a speech:

In the speech, I inserted an illiteracy rate for girls in Korea that turned out to be off by a lot. It was entirely my fault. The error created some very negative fallout. Rather than blame me in public and say something like, "She's not careful enough to be my research assistant anymore," Larry pulled me aside and said, "You messed up, you've seen the consequences, and you're not going to make a mistake like that again." People tend to doubt women more than men. So when you do mess up and your mentor still believes in you and stands behind you, it means a lot. I quadruple checked every figure I gave him after that.

Other women offered similar stories about powerful mentors who were unafraid to let them hear about it when they made mistakes or got off course, but to a man, these mentors delivered corrective feedback in private while continuing to extol their mentees' virtues in public:

> He was so incredibly tough, but he was always in my corner. So, when things did go south, whether we missed a budget or failed to implement something correctly, he might let me have an earful if I screwed up badly, but when it came to defending his team, I could not ask for a greater champion.
>
> —Susan Chambers

> Once, despite the Colonel's explicit zero-tolerance policy on drug use, I strongly supported a soldier who had failed a drug screen at a punishment hearing in front of the Colonel. I could tell he was unhappy. Rather than admonishing me in front of my people, after the hearing he dismissed everyone in the room but me. He sat me down and talked to me in a very direct way about his policy and his rationale. Because he wouldn't embarrass me publicly and because I could trust him to give me direct, critical feedback, we really respected each other, even when we didn't agree.
>
> —Becky Halstead

Here is a paradox: confronting a mentee about bad performance or unprofessional behavior may cause her some pain and distress in the short term. But it also conveys genuine care and commitment. On the other hand, avoiding critical feedback may spare her some pain in the short term while setting her up for ultimate failure. Each and every one of our interviewees emphasized the importance of her mentor providing critical feedback about her job performance—especially when something needed to improve. Kathy Waller emphasized the importance of being receptive to timely feedback and how her mentor, Peter Ueberroth, helped her:

> Very few people give you instant feedback because they have to think about how to tell you. A lot of times delaying feedback diminishes its value in helping you make changes. Men were always worried about how to tell me, until they got to that point in the relationship where they were brutally honest. Peter is now brutally honest. But in the very beginning, when I could have benefited more, he was hesitant. I think that the faster you can get to a place where you don't react to feedback, the better off you'll be.

Be her raving fan in public and her most reliable critic in private.

28. Help Her Sharpen Her Leadership Style (Don't Change It)

I often sensed that my male colleagues expected my leadership style to be very directive, commanding, and transactional. But my natural style—and that of many women—is to be more collaborative, democratic, and inclusive. So, there is a delicate balance in how I am perceived. At times, I sensed that some men thought my transformational style was "wafflely." Yet, if I was too directive as a woman, then I might be perceived as pulling rank to get what I want. I have had to work very hard to give myself permission to have my own leadership style.

—Dana Born, Brigadier General (ret)

Women often lead differently than men.

The traditionally masculine "command and control" leadership model—a model that assumes a good leader is action oriented, dominant, competitive, self-sufficient, and always willing to impose his will on others to get the job done—is proving increasingly inadequate in the modern workplace.[22] In its place, organizations are hungry for transformational leaders who score high on social and emotional intelligence, value collaboration, and stimulate creativity through inspiration. There is a growing demand for leadership infused with soft skills (e.g., empathy, caring, listening skills, approachability) as we find more team and group-focused work tasks in today's workplace.[23] It may come as no surprise then to learn that organizations with women in top positions perform better on many key success indices than organizations with primarily male leadership.[24]

Guys, let's review the behavioral styles and core values that women often bring to the task of leadership. We acknowledge up front that leadership style can vary as much among women as it does among men, yet statistical meta-analyses of hundreds of studies on gender and leadership point to some consistent themes in the techniques women prefer to get the job done.[25] We think of these as *Athena Values* in leadership.[26] Use this broad snapshot of commonly feminine leadership values as a good starting place to understand, appreciate, and then champion the rising Athenas around you. Here we go.

On the whole, gender and leadership studies show that women adopt a leadership style described as transformational, democratic (communal), and participative. In their relationships with team members, women leaders are more empathic, patient, and inclined to put others first. Feedback from peers, supervisors, and subordinates reveals that, when compared with men, women are rated higher in teamwork, empowerment, information sharing, and genuine care for all team members. And when it comes to decision making, women are more inclusive and thoughtful about the impact decisions will have on others; women often harbor a sense of responsibility and obligation to others and others' best interests. Finally, women are more likely than men to opt for praise and empathy—rather than criticism—as a catalyst for innovation, and they define winning in the plural; teams rather than individuals are given credit for success.

By now, you must be thinking, "This all sounds great, so what's the problem?" Here is the problem: many man-centric organizations—maybe yours included—don't implicitly value some of these more feminine leadership styles. This will force women you mentor into painful double binds: if a woman adopts traditionally masculine leader behaviors and becomes authoritative and dominant, "taking charge," as it were, she is actually likely to lose in three ways.[27] First, behaving like a guy may feel like a genuine violation of who she is at work. Anyone knows that pretending to be someone you're not is exhausting and, ultimately, depressing.

Second, she may feel forced to choose between being liked *or* respected (a choice men rarely have to make). Gender researcher Alice Eagly reflected that, on one hand, women are expected to deliver warmth, friendliness, compassion, and nurturing. On the other hand, they'd better take charge and behave like men (e.g., be assertive, competitive, heroic) when they lead. But simultaneously impressing others as a good leader and a good woman is neither easy nor natural.[28]

Here is the final—and perhaps most deflating—paradox for women in leadership. Even if they manage to suppress their more egalitarian leader inclinations and behave more like the men around them, they still lose! There is evidence that women who are more agentic, authoritative, and masculine in their leadership style are more likely to be disliked, sabotaged, and attacked in their careers—by both men and women.[29] Colleagues may see assertive women as presumptuous, and in male-dominated cultures they may be dismissed as "bitches" and consistently undermined.

Men, when you mentor a woman, it is crucially important to watch, listen, and learn about her unique approach to motivating and influencing those she leads. Do not assume that her approach should mimic your own. Chances are she'll feel enough pressure to suppress her own style and "fit in" with the guys' club. Instead, help her articulate her unique vision and preferred strategies for leading. Then, help create leadership opportunities for her. If her approach is working, get busy helping her to shape and sharpen it. Finally, go out of your way to draw attention to her leadership successes and push back at gender-biased criticisms or efforts to undermine her.

Oh, and don't forget to watch closely: you might learn a thing or two about leadership!

29. Be a Watchdog for Disparities at Work

When Nadine Kaslow—past president of the American Psychological Association—was promoted to the rank of full professor at Emory University, she immediately called her mentor and shared the good news:

> His first response to me was "Great! What kind of raise do you get?" I told him full professors didn't get raises at promotion. He said, "You need to go to your business manager and find out what percent raise the men got when they got promoted. Then, request in writing the mean of that amount." So, I wrote a formal request to the dean for an 8 percent raise, which was the mean raise for men promoted at that time. The dean's office then looked at my salary and it was so low that I got a 30 percent raise! That tells you how low my salary was. If my mentor had not encouraged me to do that, I never would have gotten that raise.

In our interviews with accomplished women, few themes resonated with both the persistence and emotional intensity as the call for male leaders and mentors to be acutely attuned to gender disparities in the workplace. And let us be honest here, gentlemen: these women expect much of you. For instance, it is not enough to do everything in your power to avoid gender stereotypes, prejudice, and discrimination in your own relationships with women. That is all well and good. But it is merely the start. The women you mentor also need you to address disparities in the way women are treated in your organization generally. They need to witness you boldly and courageously *saying* and *doing* something when discriminatory practices threaten not only their own prospects for success and promotion, but the prospects of women writ large. For your mentees to feel safe with you, and for your own credibility, you need to address disparities out loud and consistently.

Like Nadine Kaslow, many of the women we interviewed recalled how a male mentor addressed gendered pay disparities in a powerful way. As a junior professor, Susan Madsen had never thought to renegotiate her academic salary: "One day my mentor called me down and said,

'I just looked at your salary.' I said, I know, it's low. He said, 'No, it's wrong!' He said, 'I'm calling the provost right now and we're going to resolve this because you deserve a lot more.' He knew that two men were hired at the same time I was for $10,000 more. Within a day, my salary had gone up $10,000 and the institution back paid me as well. That meant a lot to me."

Similarly, Laura Behling has been impressed by men who consistently push for pay equity and transparency so that women are not left behind: "One of the things I've seen done very effectively when men have entered supervisor roles is to do a thorough review of job descriptions and salaries for men and women, to make sure women have not been left behind. These men openly verify that if women are doing equivalent work, that they are receiving equivalent titles, promotions, and pay in comparison to men. That can be very powerful."

Guys, you've also got to be attuned to varieties of bias and discrimination in the workplace beyond pay and benefits. For instance, women are more often exposed to personally demeaning and disrespectful coworker behavior.[30] You will find this especially true for women of color. Work on "listening" to everyday workplace exchanges with empathy for the way your female mentee might hear them. When you hear something disparaging of women, we hope you'll have the cojones to say something about it. Consider the experience of Dana Born when she was a professor at the Air Force Academy:

I recall a briefing attended by all male senior professors and leaders on the Air Force's current aircraft fleet. During the briefing, the speaker, a man, referred to one of the aircraft using profane slang that was quite derogatory toward women. I sat there thinking, he didn't just say that, did he? By the end of the meeting, my anxiety was high because I knew I had to say something, the comment was entirely inappropriate. Then, the dean came forward and said, "I want to say that some of the language used today has no place in today's Air Force. It should never be used again, either inside or outside this room." I was so relieved knowing that my boss really "got it." When the sole woman in the room doesn't have to address language that is denigrating or dismissive to women, and inappropriate, when men take charge and do that, it is very powerful.

A final category of gender disparity at work has to do with opportunities for promotion based upon equivalent work and achievement. Is your mentee the victim of the *prove-it-again bias*?[31] In addition to doing what her male peers do, does she have to jump through rings of fire or bill twice the client hours to be viewed as equally competent? Are her missteps magnified and her achievements attributed to luck? Most important, when vacancies come open and candidates for promotion are considered, is she mysteriously left off the list? Navy Admiral Michelle Howard described the critical importance of men ensuring that candidate lists for promotions include women: "If candidate lists are always 100 percent majority members, then women or diverse members will never be hired; their names are never up for consideration."

Watch for evidence of unfair treatment for women. Then do something about it.

30. Help Her Construct a Rich Constellation of Career Helpers

Here is our last nugget of wisdom for really helping a woman take off and soar professionally: for goodness sake, don't do the *guru thing*.

Guys, let's level with one another. There is still just enough of the caveman in each of us, just enough alpha-male behavior coded in our DNA, that we can instinctively and unconsciously respond to women with protectiveness and possessiveness; you know, *me Tarzan, you Jane*. In our mentorships, this means we are all vulnerable to desperately enacting the heroic guru mentor for the women we guide. Here's the problem: not only does it rarely work, it will also stunt her development and limit her ultimate success.

Kerry Ann Rockquemore, president and CEO of the National Center for Faculty Development & Diversity, recently observed that we must dispense with the traditional guru notion of mentoring that paints the mentor as the all-knowing, all-providing wise man who protects a mentee from all evil forces in the organization and meets all of her needs for support while scarcely breaking a sweat.[32] In other words, don't kid yourselves, guys! The chances that you can provide everything a woman—or a man—needs to thrive in a career are slim to none.

Gentlemen, we're providing a dose of reality here, and hopefully, taking some of the weight off your shoulders. We hope it comes as some relief to know you can't—and shouldn't try to—be all things to your mentee. The traditional guru model of mentoring is old school. It also doesn't work. The truth of it is that most of us require more than one helping relationship during important periods in our lives—and certainly throughout our careers.[33] Yes, having a primary mentor is often critical during the all-important early-career phase, especially in one's first job, but most of us benefit from a wider constellation of helping connections. These helpful collections of relationships are often described as *developmental networks, composite mentoring*, or, our favorite, *mentoring constellations*, and evidence from many career fields suggests that those who enjoy multiple sources of mentoring are more productive, successful, and content with their careers than those without such a rich constellation.[34]

Gentlemen, here is the bottom line: the wider and more comprehensive a woman's network of career helpers, the better the chances that she will succeed, not just today and not just in your organization, but later, throughout her career. Want her to soar? Then get busy helping her to construct a rich, robust, and fail-safe network of support. Here are some specific steps to take. First, deliberately introduce your mentee to the concept of a mentoring constellation, explain the benefits of multiple mentors and career helpers, and have honest conversations about your own strengths and relative weaknesses (e.g., the contours of your own experience and expertise) as a guide.

Second, as your mentorship progresses, as trust develops, and as you gain a better sense of her career ambitions, think out loud with her about other people—potential mentors—and layers of support (e.g., key members of your own network, organizations for women, online networks). In light of your own experience, strengths, and interests, who else in the organization might complement what you offer? For instance, if you're a guy without a family, it may help to connect a mentee wrestling with work–family demands with a colleague who is also navigating the challenge of young children or an aging parent. If there are very few women in your organization, perhaps you can connect your mentee with a female colleague external to the organization who can offer support and a confidential safe space for sharing gender-based challenges. Or perhaps you know a power broker in the profession who can open a key door for her on the road to achieving her unique career dream.

We conclude with a final warning about your inner caveman. Sometimes, we've seen male mentors become jealous and territorial upon learning that a female mentee is receiving career help or personal support from others. To this we ask, really, dude? Honestly, nothing will undermine a woman's efforts at developing a healthy and helpful constellation more quickly than a prickly and possessive mentor. So check your inner caveman at the door, suppress your guru tendencies, and don't you dare express hurt or anger when a mentee widens and strengthens her mentoring network. Just be satisfied to be an important part of it. It's about her, not you.

9

Matters of Personal Growth

Gentlemen, here are eight elements to excellent mentoring with women that emphasize her social and emotional development. Think of these as the *psychosocial* functions of excellent mentoring. Each of these mentoring elements will hinge upon the quality of the connection and emotional bond you manage to form with your mentee. Each element is profoundly important in shaping the course of her success as a professional—particularly in traditionally male-dominated professions and organizations. To be an outstanding mentor for a woman, you'll need to discern and then honor her unique career vision and her distinctive notion of ideal work–life balance. To do this, you'll have to acknowledge that many of the women you mentor will have more work to do outside of work than you. You've also got to build her confidence at every turn, champion her assertiveness, and fan her pursuit of excellence without slipping into the self-defeating abyss of perfectionism. A terrific mentor also challenges his mentees to take full credit for their accomplishments. Finally, a strong mentor is secure enough as a man and a mentor to help a woman integrate her professional identity with her sense of self as a woman.

31. Discern and Honor Her Career Vision

The Italian Renaissance painter, poet, and sculptor Michelangelo (1475–1564) is said to have approached his sculpting as a process of revealing and uncovering the figures hidden in stone. In social psychology, the *Michelangelo phenomenon* describes how, in close relationships, partners often sculpt each other, gently shaping the other's self and guiding the other toward the desired vision of the self.[1] As you might ascertain, the Michelangelo phenomenon—and the metaphor of the sculptor—may also describe the way in which a skilled mentor affirms the ideal and authentic self-image of a mentee. As a mentor, part of your job is to help a mentee to articulate her *ideal self*, her hopes, dreams, and aspirations. Then, each time you interact with her, consider how you can propel her closer to her ideal self. Skilled mentors do this in two important ways.[2]

First comes *perceptual affirmation*; effective mentors are intentional about slowing down and really "seeing" their mentees. Can you establish enough trust so that she will reveal her ideal self and her career dream? Take the time to understand a woman as an individual, not as merely a woman, a monolith to her gender. Among the most important mentoring gifts you can give a woman is the willingness to learn about her unique blend of interests and aspirations. If a mentor is consistently available and accessible, his mentee is likely to read caring in his manner and behavior. This in turn makes her comfortable enough to open up and share about her ideal vision of herself.

The second element of propelling a woman toward her ideal self is *behavioral affirmation*; excellent mentors help their mentees to engage in behaviors aligned with their ideal selves. Put simply, having gained a window into her unique image of the ideal—who she dreams of becoming—the mentor must help open doors and conjure the opportunities and experiences she'll require to get there.

Gentlemen, if you mentor her with the sort of patience and affirmation we describe here, your mentee will be less inclined to hide and repress her distinct talents and her ideal vision for her life. If you consistently mirror for her the person and professional she aspires to become, she will be encouraged and emboldened to go for it! And there's more: by discerning her career dream, endorsing it, and then enabling it with the right opportunities and experiences, you will contribute to her personal happiness and well-being.[3]

In the process of coming to know your mentee—carefully discerning her career/life dream—it is important to simultaneously help her look beyond her current aspirations when you see potential that she cannot.[4] Consider the reflection of Rear Admiral Sandy Stosz about her own mentors:

They gave me opportunities I hadn't thought about. They gave me a chance to look beyond what I had as my vision, which was just becoming a sailor and commanding a ship one day. They helped me look at a bigger picture, not just the Coast Guard but the entire Department of Transportation. Those two men showed me that there's more out there than just settling for going to sea, that there are special jobs and possibilities I hadn't even considered.

An effective mentor can see new and better possibilities for a mentee. Are there opportunities available to her (personal or professional) that she has never dared to consider? Is her current self-vision limited by her history with nay-saying family members or her own struggles with self-confidence? If so, it is up to you to find ways to empower her to entertain a bolder vision. At times, it will be up to you to cast a more audacious vision of where she can go and who she can become. Then, communicate unshakable belief in her ability to get there.

We now come full circle. As Michelangelo almost certainly would have reminded you: it is fine to cast new and inspiring visions for your mentee. But in the end, you've got to honor her decisions. Inspire and empower her, but don't pressure her to take jobs or seek promotions that don't call to her. The research evidence is clear. Women often report deep satisfaction from jobs that provide personal meaning, authenticity, and balance between life and relationships.[5] Frankly, her identity may be less tied to lockstep promotions or positional prestige.

Like a thoughtful sculptor, help her discern and then affirm her ideal vision of self. If she seems to be aiming low or selling herself short, paint a more ambitious vision of her potential, including previously uncontemplated possibilities. Then, communicate unconditional support for her right to choose her ideal career destination and vigorously champion her efforts to get there.

32. Remember, She (Probably) Has More Work Outside of Work Than You

Research on stress among graduate students shows that female grad students are significantly more likely than their male counterparts to experience conflicts resulting from their roles external to graduate school (e.g., spouse, parent, caregiver to an older parent, employee).[6] More often than men, female grad students report symptoms of stress, anxiety, and depression from having to juggle childcare, outside employment, and the lion's share of domestic chores around the home. When resources (e.g., time and energy) are overcome by demands, conflict occurs, with associated outcomes of stress, role dissatisfaction, and, potentially, role exit (she ditches her advanced degree aspirations altogether).[7] And it doesn't get any easier. Early career studies reveal that these role tensions persist for women once they enter the workforce. For instance, women in science and technology report intense expectations to combine demanding personal and professional lives without allowing either to be affected by the stress—and, sometimes, the flat-out absurdity—of trying to be both high-flying scientist and engaged, available parent.[8]

Here's the problem: guys often continue to get a pass on having a significant presence at home. If a guy's kicking ass and taking names on his way up the ladder at work, well, does it really matter how much of the burden he shares at home? After all, that's what wives are for. But if a woman has a career and a family, organizations—and sometimes the male mentors within them—fail to account for the fact that she'll quite often have more work to do at home than her same-rank male peers. Laura Behling, dean and provost at Knox College, observed that: "Some men in mentoring positions still lack awareness that some women have to lead separate lives outside of their work environment. Sometimes, there are expectations on women for childcare or eldercare that men may not have."

So how are your female mentee's demands outside of work relevant to your mentorship? First, it can be very difficult for a woman facing difficulties or exhaustion juggling work–family demands to relate to a male role model who just doesn't get it; he either hasn't had to carry this kind of burden or doesn't seem interested in understanding or showing empathy for her experience.[9] Gentlemen, you've got to stop and reorient when mentoring a woman, especially in a male-dominated work environment. Over time, your relationship with her should help build her resiliency and her capacity to handle stress—including work–life demands—but your relationship won't get out of the blocks if you don't work on your compassion and genuine understanding when challenges from her life external to work spill over to her self-efficacy and engagement on the job.

Guys, you don't need to have experienced her unique demands for care of children, parents, or other domestic obligations to be concerned and caring when she shares her experience with you. And by all means, when you slip, forget, and behave as though her career should be her only concern, be sure to man up and apologize. Again, a spot-on recommendation from Laura Behling: "For men, sometimes the default is, 'Why can't we stay late and work till six or seven tonight?' Well, sometimes, she actually can't! So, I would say a good mentor will acknowledge this oversight right away with something like, 'Oh, of course, I never should have assumed.' He should own his wrong assumption."

33. Honor Her Approach to Work–Life Balance

Women frequently express a desire for mentoring that integrates career and family dimensions of life. Often, the contour between work and life is more permeable for women. Your male colleagues and mentees may be able to simply "turn off" spouse and parent roles when they arrive at work each day. Women? Not so much. As we established in element 32, women often balance greater obligations for children and family while striving to excel professionally. They may also enter the workforce later than men and they are more likely to interrupt their career paths—at least intermittently—to attend to childcare or other family responsibilities.[10] Guys, if talking with your female mentees about finding the "right" work–life balance falls outside your comfort zone, you've really got to get over it. Many of the women you mentor will prize these conversations.

Research on mentoring outcomes reveals that when mentoring is inclusive of career *and* family, women are more likely to experience a range of positive behavioral, attitudinal, motivational, and even health-related outcomes.[11] Betsy Myers discovered that this inclusivity was a key ingredient in her mentorship with Warren Bennis: "Warren is someone I talked to about my life across the spectrum. It wasn't just my book or my leadership work, I talked to Warren about my family, my personal life, difficulties I encountered in my marriage or parenting; I could talk to him about anything. I've had those kinds of relationships with mentors. Life is not just about business, it's about these other big dimensions of our lives."

Gentlemen, here's the thing about work–life balance: the "right" allocation of time and energy between work and life external to work will be different for every woman you mentor. Don't make an ass of yourself and *ass*ume she'll share your own work–life priorities or that because she's a woman, she'll choose to step away from her career to have children. In science and technology, for example, some senior women tend to "look" precisely like many of their male counterparts in terms of valuing work and career relative to family, while others find alternative niches in the sciences that allow for greater balance between work and nonwork life.[12]

And here is another wrinkle: expect your female mentees to experience different work–life balance concerns at each stage of life and career.[13] Decisions about whether to get married, whether to have children (and when), how to arrange childcare, whether to work part or full time, and whether to become primary caregiver for a parent may all loom large for your mentees at different stops along their careers, each bringing moments of conflict, and each demanding your listening ear, understanding, and support. And don't forget to allocate separate reserves of empathy for women who launch or restart careers in midlife—perhaps after children enter school or depart for college. New midlife mentees bring a unique set of concerns to the workplace. These may include concerns about shifting roles as parent, spouse, and child; feelings of emptiness or loss; a sense of isolation and uniqueness; and insecurity—the dreaded *imposter syndrome*—regarding competence.

Here are some of the key values and experiences women often report when working through decisions about how to balance a career with family commitments.[14] First, they define success—both life and career—in terms of intrinsically rewarding roles, self-development, balance, *and* career achievement (it's not just about financial compensation or moving up the corporate ladder). Second, satisfaction in interpersonal relationships is a salient predictor of happiness, at work and at home; dysfunctional relationships in either venue may take a serious toll on a woman's health and happiness. Third, women often report colliding with the *maternal wall* when they arrive at the decision to have children;[15] the choice to have children elicits questions about a woman's competence and her commitment to do the job. Moreover, women—far more than men—exit work when a child is born, often because the workplace feels toxic and inflexible.

In summary, gentlemen, here are some key strategies for honoring your mentee's unique work–life balance concerns and inclinations:

♦ It is essential that you communicate interest and openness to discussing and brainstorming her preferences and creative strategies for work–life balance—but for goodness' sake, don't be intrusive or creepy about it! Be open and prepared when she's ready to share.

♦ Help her to normalize and de-catastrophize common pressures and conflicts associated with juggling family and career. Dana Born of Harvard University encourages men to be matter-of-fact and unruffled when female mentees experience tribulation balancing roles. Your equanimity and steady support will be grounding and deeply encouraging.

♦ Encourage her to find her unique rhythm when it comes to work and life. Marissa Mayer, CEO of Yahoo, empowers her employees to find the "merge," the work–life solution that allows excellent employees to be with their children without ending their careers.

♦ Be an advocate for workplace policies that allow women—and men—latitude and flexibility to work hard and take time away for family.

34. Take Every Opportunity to Build Her Confidence

When Air Force Brigadier General (ret) Dana Born was a comparatively new professor and a department chair at the Air Force Academy, the dean of faculty position came open. Though Born was reticent, her longtime mentor (a more senior professor) urged her to apply. Born said,

"Despite my misgivings, that I wasn't ready, wasn't seasoned or experienced enough, he convinced me that I was both ready *and* the right person for the job. He asked me the proverbial question, 'If not now, when?' He even arranged a mock practice interview in which he acted as the Secretary of the Air Force to prepare me for the real thing."

Guys, be persistent in promoting self-confidence—a strong sense of self-in-the-profession—in the women you mentor. *Self-confidence* is simply belief in oneself and one's prowess or abilities. There is a clear link between self-confidence and career satisfaction, promotion rate, and income.[16] Not surprisingly, the more attention and assistance one receives from a mentor, the greater one's confidence and *career self-efficacy*: the extent to which a person believes she is capable of successfully managing her career and succeeding in the future.[17]

Four decades ago, pioneering psychologist Albert Bandura discovered that people who believe they can perform well (those with high self-efficacy) are significantly more likely to tackle a difficult task and persist longer at that task than someone with lower self-efficacy.[18] The stronger your mentee's confidence, the more obstacles—at work and in life—will stimulate her to stay in the fight and try harder, versus giving up in a cloud of discouragement. If you can bolster her self-efficacy, momentary setbacks will quickly be forgotten. She'll be less prone to personalize and worry about failure if she has no doubt that your approval and support are unconditional.

Particularly in male-dominated professions, the environment for women can feel exclusionary, marginalizing, and persistently discriminating, elements that take a toll on a woman's psychological well-being—especially her confidence and self-efficacy. Here is the good news, gentlemen: you can help counteract these confidence-draining forces by deliberately taking every opportunity—and there will be *lots* of them—to restore and expand her confidence, hope, optimism, and resilience.[19] Bolster her self-confidence by providing copious doses of acceptance, confirmation, admiration, and emotional support.

Here's the thing. When you express consistent confidence and positive regard for her—and her work—she will be increasingly likely to adopt your positive view of her as valid.[20] A well-mentored person will increasingly embrace the *possible self*—an image of what one can become in life and in the profession—conveyed by the patient and affirming mentor.[21] Susan Madsen described one powerful technique employed by her own mentor to bolster her self-confidence: "With him, I could just tell he had confidence in me because he kept asking me to do important things. He would pull me aside and tell me that he needed input on a particular matter. I would give him feedback and then he would actually go do it! I was like, wow, I have a lot of influence already because he really trusts me."

Here is another technique for building your mentee's confidence. Take frequent opportunities to narrate and reflect upon both small improvements and big milestones. If she is struggling with self-confidence and feeling like an imposter, she may have tunnel vision, seeing only the hurdles ahead while missing evidence of achievement and hurdles cleared.[22] Point out and applaud the risks she has taken and affirm increasing evidence of her competency in various work domains.

Gentlemen, we can promise you that if you are attentive, kind, and persistent in narrating her achievements and expressing unwavering belief in her potential, your contribution to her self-efficacy will be permanently etched in her positive sense of self. In fact, the impact of a mentor on the personal esteem and confidence of a mentee often endures even after death.[23] Research shows that deceased mentors continue to influence mentees for the better; images and memories of the mentor's affirmation often buoy a mentee when times get tough.

35. Encourage Excellence but Challenge Perfectionism

Outstanding mentors understand the critical importance of communicating high—not unrealistic—expectations of mentees. When a mentor persistently voices high expectations and communicates confidence that the mentee can deliver, the stage is set for exceptional performance. Termed the *Pygmalion effect* in the psychology of leadership, the phenomenon of high expectation resulting in better performance is now well established.[24] For instance, in the original study of this effect, psychologists Robert Rosenthal and Lenore Jacobson showed that if teachers were led to expect high performance from certain children, then sure enough, those children performed at a higher level.[25]

Here's the thing, guys: if your mentee can't count on you, her mentor, to cast an inspiring vision of her promise and potential in the profession, who *can* she count on? Don't be timid when it comes to expressing an ambitious picture of just how well she can perform and how high she can soar. And be kind but impeccably honest in providing corrective feedback, especially when her effort seems haphazard. The U.S. Army slogan that inspired a generation—*Be all you can be!*—should become your mentoring mantra. Should you fail to signal high expectations and encourage her best work, you might just be guilty of creating the dreaded *golem effect* in your mentee, a psychological phenomenon—the diametric opposite of the *Pygmalion effect*—in which lower expectations by a mentor lead to poorer performance by the mentee.[26]

As you might surmise, promoting excellence and stimulating top performance in your mentee is a delicate undertaking. It is a paradox that many of the women who will be most delightful for you to mentor—high-achieving, self-motivated, determined, capable—will also be the very women most vulnerable to unrealistic, perfectionistic self-demands. *Perfectionism* in a mentee will be apparent in these behaviors: striving for flawlessness, setting excessive—even inhuman—performance standards, making painfully critical self-evaluations, and showing persistent anxiety about failure or perhaps even disappointing you as a mentor. Cognitive psychologists know that perfectionism is a script for self-defeat. Sure, perfectionistic self-demands can drive behavior, but in the end, they tend to undermine success. The perfectionist frequently becomes so fearful of failure that procrastination (*If I can't be assured of doing it perfectly, I can't do it*) sets in. If your mentee is internally terrified of failure and/or your disapproval, she may put off tasks and challenges, ensuring failure. She might also become obsessive about small mistakes or setbacks and might ultimately default to evaluating herself in black and white terms: *do it perfectly or be a worthless failure.*

So, how can you gracefully walk the line between excellence and perfectionism in your mentoring work? Here are some key strategies to put into practice. First, be a role model for imperfection. Be comfortable in your own skin and show her that *even you*, her wise and accomplished mentor, sometimes get it wrong, make mistakes, and feel anxious.

Above all, do what men around the globe often fear doing: be honest when you don't know something. Ask for directions if you are lost, and point out when you get something wrong. Don't be that dude who can't tolerate admitting he doesn't know it all. For goodness' sake, if you have to, practice saying, "I don't know," in front of the mirror so that you are comfortable being imperfect while also refusing to denigrate yourself for it. Be deliberate about showing her that competent people—starting with you—are entirely imperfect.

Second, directly, but humorously, challenge perfectionistic thinking. When your mentee overreacts to an oversight, error, or subpar performance, perhaps with emotional distress and extreme self-downing (e.g., *I'm such an idiot, I'll never get this right, I'm in over my head, I'm thinking of quitting*), be patient, understanding, and willing to use humor to show her the futility of perfectionism and get her back on track (e.g., *What? You mean you're not perfect? I never would have agreed to mentor you if I'd had any idea you were a human being!!!*).

36. Champion Her Assertiveness

Women walk a tightrope.

When men are assertive—sometimes, even aggressive—at work, more often than not, onlookers think to themselves, *what a strong leader!* But when a woman is equally assertive? Not so much. Like other women, those you mentor may find themselves teetering on a precarious edge.[27] Lean too far one direction (feminine, warm, likeable) and they may be treated kindly but not taken seriously and quickly dismissed to the junior varsity. But, lean too far the other way (traditionally masculine, assertive, directive) and they are labeled harsh, unpleasant, and socially unskilled, and rejected as "bitches" and "ballbusters."

Gentlemen, you've got to be attuned to your mentees' struggle to find balance on the assertiveness tightrope. Although guys lean in the direction of bravado and overconfidence in their own performance, evidence suggests that women are generally more modest and subdued in their self-assessments.[28] In *Lean In*, Sheryl Sandberg observes that, thanks to societal expectations of girls, women can feel reluctant about taking risks and firmly advocating for themselves.[29] After all, like men, they have been brought up to see men as strong, independent, and assertive while women are gentle, deferential, and modest.

As a mentor, it is up to you to empower the women you mentor to stick up for themselves, speak the truth clearly, and stand by their decisions. Sometimes, merely having the firm backing and encouragement of a mentor is just the green light a mentee might require to begin making her perspective clear and her voice heard. Consider the experience of Nadine Kaslow, when, as a very junior psychologist, she was invited to attend a grant review meeting with her mentor:

> I essentially kept quiet in the meeting, despite having a much more favorable opinion of a grant proposal than a very famous psychologist in the room. I didn't have the confidence to speak up and argue for the proposal. At the next break, I came out of the bathroom and my mentor was standing there. He said, "Don't you ever do that again. You just hurt someone's career because you didn't have the courage to speak up to someone famous." Well, I needed that. I was not assertive enough and, personally, I needed that permission.

It may also be useful to cheerlead her assertiveness in historically male-dominated workplaces where chauvinistic, rude, abrasive male behavior persists.[30] If she has been socialized to overlook or gloss over misogynist and abusive male behavior, it is essential that—in addition to addressing such toxic behavior yourself—you work with her to find an assertive voice that is uniquely hers, an approach that puts the bad actors on notice while allowing her to preserve those traditionally feminine elements of her leadership style (e.g., collaboration, cooperation, kindness) that she most values.

And don't forget to encourage her to be deliberate and assertive about asking for help and constructing a rich constellation of mentors and sponsors (see element 30). Once again, women, more than men, may have been socialized to wait for potential mentors to notice them. Former White House advisor Betsy Myers discovered this to be true: "As women, too often we just put our head down and hope that someone notices. Sometimes, I don't think women are as strategic as they should be about the relationships they need to succeed. Sometimes, we don't ask; we don't nurture those relationships, to our detriment. Women have got to take responsibility for developing the relationships with the people in the organization who can make a difference."

Here are some final keys to championing your mentee's assertive behavior:

♦ *Watch your own gender bias*: Even well-meaning male mentors may find themselves reflecting to women: "It's nice that you are more assertive, but don't be too aggressive!" when the very behavior that elicited that comment would never be uttered to a male mentee.[31] If your mentee's assertiveness makes you uncomfortable, get over it—don't confirm the stereotype that behavior that's assertive in a man is aggressive in a woman.

♦ *Don't assume that assertiveness will be a problem for her*: Many of the women you mentor will be quite adept at asserting their will and voicing their opinions clearly and confidently. In this case, smile, nod, and give them the thumbs up. Only when you detect that greater assertiveness will be necessary for her to get noticed and garner respect will you need to shape and reinforce increasingly firm and self-assured behavior.

♦ *Remember to let her be assertive her way*: Many women discover a unique sweet spot in balancing femininity and assertiveness. For example, the "little bit of sugar" strategy works for some women who prefer to combine politeness with firmness in negotiating to get their own needs met at work.[32] When it comes to assertiveness, if it ain't broke, don't try to fix it! Champion her approach if it works for her.

37. Challenge Her to Take Full Credit for Her Accomplishments

News flash, gentlemen: women you mentor may be dismissed, overlooked, and disadvantaged at work simply because they are less likely than men to take full credit for their hard work and achievements. Once again, gender differences and socialization are implicated. Because women can suffer the *impostor syndrome* at work, even high-achieving women can feel they're not deserving of the success they encounter. And because many women find more identity and meaning in connection to others rather than merely individual triumphs, they too quickly give credit for their accomplishments to others in their work groups—especially men.[33]

Consider the results from a disconcerting but perfectly illustrative series of studies from the *Personality and Social Psychology Bulletin*.[34] This research revealed that, in the workplace, women who work with men are significantly less likely to take credit for their work than those who collaborate with other women. Working in mixed-gender teams, women give more credit than is necessary—or even accurate—to their male colleagues. Guys, if you're mentoring a woman, this finding should alarm you. Be alert to the possibility that when your mentee is paired with male partners, she'll devalue her own contributions and divert the credit to others, specifically, the men in the group.

The problem, of course, is that if she demurs and defers credit too often, she'll be discounted, undercompensated, and, very likely, exploited by the guys in the workplace who are taking unfair credit for her hard work. Your mission—should you choose to accept it—is to get her to talk about herself in an honest way, taking credit where credit is due. It's perfectly fine for her to talk about her great team and trumpet their collaborative efforts; after all, that signifies excellent leadership. But don't let her give so much credit that she hides her own contributions. When you give her high praise for her work, point out if she shies away from accepting it or shifts the recognition to anyone but herself. Then, challenge her to simply say, "Thank you."

In our interview with Kathy Hannan, she offered a poignant example of how an alert mentor can helpfully bring the problem with deferring credit to the attention of a mentee:

One night, I was working late and he walked into my work area and asked me if I thought I was doing a good job. I said I was doing a pretty good job. He then asked if I thought a male colleague was doing a good job. Now I felt out of my comfort zone.

Then, he asked me if I was doing a better job than this male colleague. I couldn't do it—even though I knew I was working harder and doing a better job than this guy—I didn't feel comfortable saying so. He then informed me that this same male colleague was telling others that he was doing all the work, taking all the credit for my work. My mentor was letting me know in clear terms that I needed to start fighting for what was mine, taking ownership and credit and communicating it. He wanted me to tell my story and get the recognition I deserved.

To mentor a woman effectively, you've got to call out her achievements and praise her great work publicly. But just as often, you've got to challenge her to take ownership for her successes and her tangible contributions to group work. Remember, she may not even be aware she tends to defer credit; it's on you to point it out to her in a way she can understand without framing it as a weakness. Help her see how claiming credit for her work will be a requirement for advancement and equal pay.

Finally, gentlemen, never forget that your mentorship with a woman may pull for this same feminine tendency to give credit to others. Research reveals that women are far more likely than men to credit their family, spouses, and *mentors* for their life and career successes.[35] When she credits your support for her successes or promotions, always pause, express sincere thanks, but then highlight in no uncertain terms how *she* deserves the lion's share of the credit and explain exactly why.

Use your mentorship as a practice field for taking appropriate credit!

38. Affirm Both Her Professional Identity and Her Sense of Self As a Woman

Each summer, on Induction Day at the U.S. Naval Academy, roughly three hundred young women enter a storied and historically all-male military service academy. Their hair is cut shorter than most of them have ever seen it, jewelry and makeup are stowed away, and they are issued uniforms that hide much of their feminine form, making them hard to distinguish from the nine hundred men around them. Over the ensuing days and weeks, they will grow accustomed to a persistent sheen of sweat as they exercise, tackle obstacle courses, and run or march constantly throughout the smoldering mid-Atlantic summer. By summer's end, these new Naval Academy women just might look in the mirror and wonder if they will ever look and feel feminine again.

In male-dominated professions such as the military, business, science, and technology, the appearance of a woman in the workplace may be an anomaly. She herself may feel unnatural and unfeminine. And if she tries to "be a guy" in most ways in order to fit in, chances are she will still be marginalized as males whisper about her likely sexual orientation and unattractiveness.[36]

To mentor women effectively, men have got to pay attention to the dilemma many women feel about having to choose between their feminine and professional identities.

Guys, women face an unsettling internal tug-of-war that few of us ever have to confront. In professions and organizations with strong masculine traditions, women may feel compelled to choose between: (a) full assimilation into male culture (aka, behaving like a guy) and (b) insisting on preserving strongly feminine habits and traditions.[37] Worse, many of these women report feeling forced to choose sides between these two groups. Women can easily find themselves in conflict with female colleagues who have chosen a different path. And there is more: female university faculty in traditionally male disciplines describe feeling forced to choose between being attractive *or* being smart.[38] These professors often report that when men do recognize and accept them for their academic worth, it often comes at the expense of their sense of selves as women.

Here's another issue we as men don't have to contend with professionally: maintaining a professional identity when our marriage status changes. Professional women, especially in male-centric professions and among dual-career couples, often find it personally meaningful and professionally strategic to maintain their surname or to adopt their married name only if hyphenated with their surname.[39] Realize that your mentee may have spent years building a professional reputation and that when she marries, retaining her name allows her to continue leveraging her hard-earned social capital. Her professional identity is important to her self-worth, her confidence, and her sense of belonging in her profession. As her mentor, your job is to help her build and then protect that identity. When a woman changes her name, her credibility as a committed member of the organization can take a hit. If she asks you, openly discuss the pros and cons of surnames and married names in the workplace. Ultimately, respect and fully support her decision.

Men, all of us who mentor women need to be sensitive to their struggles to assimilate into predominantly male workplaces. How can you do this? Make your mentorship a *safe space* for her to wrestle out loud with her experiences and provide validation and support as she works to develop an authentic and "right fit" balance between the feminine and professional elements of her identity.[40] As you listen to her, be particularly attentive to times when valued components of her identity (e.g., professional, team member, spouse, parent) are not fully valued in the workplace. Make sure that the mentoring relationship is a place where her full identity can be shared, acknowledged, and strongly affirmed. If she feels forced to choose between being a competent professional and being a woman—in all the ways her gender identity is important to her—then by all means, you'd better show her you are comfortable discussing this with her. Listen carefully, empathize, validate her full identity as a woman *and* as a competent professional, and then help her discern a way forward that allows her to honor this integrated identity.

10

What Not to Do

Gentlemen, this final chapter contains eight elements that address some of the most pressing things you must always remember *not* to do as a mentor for a woman. These elements are designed to spare you both minor oversights and cataclysmic blunders in the mentor role. They are also written with your mentee's best interests at heart. By carefully attending to each of these cautions, you are less likely to undermine a potentially helpful developmental relationship with a woman.

Good mentors for women are egalitarian, not dominant and overbearing. They honor their mentees' unique approach to balancing reason with emotion. Although they are eager to push their mentees forward for career opportunities and job promotions, they are careful to do so only when their mentees demonstrate sufficient competence to succeed at the next level. They are alert and attuned to benignly sexist behavior and they are vigilant to avoid efforts to clone themselves and their careers in their mentees. Of course, competent male mentors are self-aware and honest with themselves about romantic and sexual feelings if these arise in a mentorship. They watch for specific red flags and take appropriate steps to avoid sexualizing mentorships. Finally, thoughtful mentors are transparent about their relationships with female mentees; they never attempt to hide these relationships from their spouses or partners.

39. Don't Be Dominant and Overbearing

Few things are as toxic as a bullying mentor.

In her study of the dark side of mentorship, Professor Terri Scandura discovered that some dysfunctional mentorships were attributed to a particularly noxious mentor type: the bullying, exploitive, egocentric mentor.[1] Often, these bullies are men. Some of these guys are flaming narcissists, egomaniacally driven to prove they're the best; they demand reverence and deference. Fail to stroke this guy's ego and you might just be the unfortunate recipient of his narcissistic rage. Other bullies erroneously equate masculinity with dominance. These—paradoxically fragile and insecure—men lead by asserting power and threatening subordinates with punishment. Women we interviewed were consistently repelled by overbearing and dominant men. Alice Eagly, an eminent professor at Northwestern University, acknowledged, "I've always avoided overbearing men. The dominant types make me feel anxious. This sort of man thinks, 'I know what she needs and I will help her get there, she just has to do what I tell her!'"

Gentlemen, your mentorship with a woman is no place for posturing, dominance, or bullying tactics (actually, we can't think of *any* relationship where these behaviors are desirable). Mentoring relationships are inherently power-unequal relationships, especially early on. Accept it. You are more experienced, often higher ranking, and, if you are serving in any supervisory capacity, a gatekeeper to key organizational rewards. The potential for abuse of power is always lurking in a man's mentorship with a woman. Here's the problem: based exclusively upon gender, women have historically been in *power-down* relationships with men. Throughout much of human history, men have literally "owned" women. A legacy of ownership, property, and male-to-female dominance are simply part of the historical narrative we bring to any male mentor–female mentee relationship. Although male privilege might still echo in our DNA and be reinforced by cultural and family traditions, we all need to be alert to avoiding behaviors that might cue outdated scripts that women *should*, *must*, or *ought to* do as we say.

Guys, if your interpersonal demeanor with a female mentee is hierarchical, domineering, and directive you can easily trigger a submissive reaction—your mentee might just retreat to socialized deference in exchange for your protection and resourcing. In order to get along, she'll follow your directives but hide her aspirations. She'll also mute her unique talents, perhaps for fear of outshining you. Of course, this will utterly stunt her professional development, not to mention her self-confidence. She might just withdraw from the relationship, wisely discerning that you don't have the essential emotional intelligence to serve as a safe guide and champion for her development as a respected colleague. Or, if she is more seasoned, more self-confident, and assertive, she might just flip you the bird. If she does, we applaud her! Listen to U.S. Army Major General Camille Nichols as she describes a situation in which a self-proclaimed mentor's overbearing demeanor created career challenges:

> One General Officer saw himself as my mentor—I did not. He moved me to a place that was very difficult for me to work. He picked me for the job to show people he wasn't "anti-women," when in fact he really was anti-women. When it was time for slating of Colonels for their next acquisition jobs, I was hinting to him that there were jobs that I would love and he wouldn't even listen to me. He put me in this position working on programs I had never worked on and that were not very important for the Army. I had to go out of my way to show how I was actually much more capable.

If you're a guy who needs to tell women what to do and demand their compliance with your directives, get out of the mentoring business.

40. Don't Make Her Choose Between Reason and Emotion

Men and women often "do emotions" differently. This evolved sex difference is now well established in the research literature.[2] For instance, men are more inclined to express anger than women and women are more likely to experience negative emotions such as guilt, embarrassment, and social anxiety. Yet, on the whole, women are more attuned (sensitive, empathic, and responsive) to the emotions of others. This means that they'd score higher than men on many indicators of emotional intelligence.

Gentlemen, one of the things we often hear from women in male-centric organizations is that they feel forced to mask or altogether recuse their well-honed empathy, their capacity for feeling and expressing emotion. The message can be subtle or blunt, but women hear it loud and clear: *leave your emotions at the door, turn off the tears, and act like a man!* When women receive this message, it has far more to do with a man's discomfort with emotion than anything else.

As a mentor, it is imperative that you honor your female mentee's unique approach to reading, expressing, and integrating feeling and emotion into her work. If she cries now and then (see element 18), if she has a gentler approach to delivering bad news, or if she is more attuned and sensitive to relational nuances than you, chalk it up to her unique emotional intelligence, not a deficit in her ability to act like a dude. Let's face it: it's not her job to make you feel comfortable with expression of emotion. It's your job to discern and honor her approach. And don't forget, mentoring is a two-way relationship; if you learn something from her about how to read emotions and interact with a more emotionally expressive coworker—good for you!

Remember, there is not a single rational or evidence-based reason to make women behave more like men when it comes to emotion. Earlier in this guide, we showed you that more feminine and egalitarian organizations—environments in which emotion, intelligence, and leadership mingle freely—are more successful and competitive for the long haul. As you mentor women, practice these crucial mentor behaviors:

1. Never assume that because she's a woman her approach to expressing emotion will be problematic. Every woman—and man—will experience and express emotions differently, and in different contexts. Be attuned and learn about her unique style of blending emotion with reason at work.

2. Never convey shame, embarrassment, or discomfort if she expresses emotion more openly and freely than you. Own the fact that it's your own discomfort that needs work, not her manner of expression.

3. If there are elements of her emotional style that seem to consistently lead to resistance from others or failure at specific tasks, discuss these honestly and strategize how she might tweak her delivery to get the intended results without sacrificing the value she places on emotional congruence.

41. Don't Misinterpret Her Reticence About Promotions

Robert Lightfoot is the chief operations officer at NASA. He is a prolific mentor to women, including Janet Petro, deputy director of the Kennedy Space Center. Over the years, Lightfoot has observed something interesting about the women he mentors: they sometimes appear hesitant and reluctant about promotions and career opportunities. Lightfoot told us:

> Women are often more honest and open about their self-doubts. They are more transparent about their insecurities regarding their qualifications. I don't see this as often with men. When I mention the next big job in a man's career trajectory, I'll often get, "Yep, sounds great, I'm ready! When do I start?" Of course, when these men walk out the door, they have the same self-doubts and worries that women have, they just don't share them. Actually, it can make mentoring harder because they won't talk to you about whether they're really ready.

Lightfoot has discovered that this trend in female transparency and honesty also holds true in job interviews: "I always ask candidates about three relative weaknesses. That question tends to reveal a lot about men and women. Women are more self-aware but also more self-critical."

Lightfoot's observation about the way some women may balk when you suggest they toss their hat in the ring for the next big career opportunity or promotion aligns with research on gender differences.[3] Women are often socialized to be more self-effacing and modest, and to report less interest in serving in leadership roles, particularly when they have just been reminded of their gender or stereotypes about women. Women also employ less bravado and puffery in estimating and discussing their skills and competence. Opportunities that come with risk of potential failure can also be particularly scary for women, especially in male-dominated workplaces, contexts where women have failed before.[4] Be sensitive to this trend if your mentee appears overly conservative when it comes to her qualifications for that next big step. In general, women are simply more honest *and* accurate in self-reporting their qualifications for a task.

Gentlemen, here is the takeaway: *do not* misinterpret your mentee's self-doubt, reservation, or hesitation when you push her forward for a next career step. If she gives voice to anxiety or insecurity about being qualified or ready, you should express admiration for her self-awareness and transparency. But don't misinterpret her hesitation as evidence she doesn't want the promotion! Understand that she might express more doubt, and appreciate that she might be more self-critical. Be patient and willing to spend time processing her concerns; have that conversation— or several—to allay her worries about whether she is qualified. Then, let her know in clear and confident terms why you believe she *is* the right person for the job and why exactly she *is* ready to step up to the next leadership tier. To mentor her well, you've got to be direct and intentional about convincing her she's ready and right for the next promotion or job.

Last, don't think your work is done once she agrees to apply for the next promotion. Sometimes, your stalwart moral support and encouragement will be necessary even when she succeeds in being selected! We conclude this element with an illustrative example, again from Robert Lightfoot's experience:

> I recall very well one female mentee who was so remarkably talented as a leader, but I had to literally convince her over and over again to apply for a major director position. Of course, once she was convinced, she was selected hands down, she just blew the interview away. When I called her in and told her she'd been selected, she put her head down and said, "Oh no..." Now, I

have just never seen a male do that! So, to be an effective mentor, I needed to continue supporting and affirming her, confronting her self-doubts even after she was chosen!

42. Don't Promote Her Before She's Ready (Benign Sabotage)

If you've just finished reading element 41, chances are you're fired up to get out there and recommend the women you mentor for key assignments or next promotions. This is all good, and we applaud your enthusiasm. But hold on just one moment. There is a caveat when it comes to convincing a woman to take the next step and compete for a promotion: don't push her forward if she's not prepared to succeed. You've got to discern the difference between a woman's socialized hesitancy and insecurity about the next big job and genuine evidence that she lacks the knowledge or skill set to perform effectively at the next level.

Promoting your mentee publicly and pressuring her privately to compete for jobs prematurely may actually set her up for failure. Gentlemen, this is *benign sabotage*. Particularly when women are a rare commodity in an organization, you may feel pressure to push your mentee up the chain as quickly as possible.[5] But if you push her forward before she's prepared, before she's had an opportunity to demonstrate sufficient competency and learn enough about the organization, you might inadvertently torpedo her success. Consider this reflection from Alice Eagly, distinguished professor at Northwestern University: "I was sometimes put forward for things too early because some men wanted to affirm and promote women. It's a sort of benevolent mentoring that can backfire. Reaching out to women to promote them to important positions is noble, but men must be careful about thinking, 'Oh! There's a great young woman! I'll put her forward for ____ promotion!' Especially if she's not ready; it may undermine her ultimate advancement."

Gentlemen, the decision to promote your mentee, encouraging her to step forward and raise her hand for advancement, is a delicate one. It demands considerable wisdom on your part as you balance two competing "goods." On one hand, it is good to champion, encourage, and promote your mentee. On the other hand, it is good to be objective in assessing her experience, skills, and motivation and how these jibe with the demands of a new job. Remember element 1: Do No Harm. If you've become smitten with a rising Athena, a talented female mentee, your objectivity may be compromised and you may find yourself compelled to put her forward prematurely. If you do, and if she crashes and burns, you own some of the blame.

Outstanding mentors champion their mentees for career-enhancing opportunities and promotions, but only when they are confident their mentees are well prepared and likely to succeed.

43. Don't Be a Benevolent Sexist

Women are wonderful, beautiful, delicate creatures. They just need a good man, a chivalrous guy, to protect, shelter, and, when necessary, rescue them from the trials and tribulations that life and career can bring.

Read the sentences above several times. They sound positive, right? I mean, women *are* great; who can argue with that? And who's going to knock a man willing to be gallant, courteous, and brave hearted when it comes to protecting a lady? Here's the problem, gentlemen: the sentence above drips with *benevolent sexism*. In 1996, Peter Glick and Susan Fiske popularized the term.[6] Benevolent sexism refers to men's evaluations of the feminine gender that may appear subjectively positive, but that are actually damaging to women and gender equality more broadly. Benevolent sexism is that magnanimous and courtly attitude toward women that we guys have perfected since our days learning about girls on the playground and receiving gender lessons from older men in our lives. Positive on the surface, benevolent sexism is actually sexist because it casts women as weak creatures in need of men's protection.

In their research, Glick and Fiske identified two distinct types of sexist male behavior.[7] *Hostile sexism* is more obvious; it describes the angry, explicitly negative attitudes toward women that often emerge when women first enter a profession or organization. Though toxic and difficult for women, hostile sexism is at least overt; a woman can see it coming and gird herself for the battle ahead. *Benevolent sexism* is more insidious but equally detrimental. Here, men view women stereotypically, benevolently endorsing them for very restricted roles but with a kind, even pandering tone (e.g., *She's a sweet young woman*; *Let's start her slowly so she doesn't get overwhelmed*). Superficially positive, benevolent sexism substitutes affection, idealization, and protectiveness for genuine respect. Such sexist attitudes justify women's subordinate status vis-à-vis men. In male-dominated organizations and professions, it also creates damaging stereotypes that women are too weak and sensitive to make it without copious hand-holding and backup support.

Benevolently sexist attitudes toward women are dangerously subtle, and may exist even among guys who view themselves as advocates for women. For instance, too many men believe women deserve a fair shot at work, just as long as men don't have to work for them.[8] Men can be reluctant about supporting women for leadership roles. Second Lieutenant Virginia Brodie related a perfect illustration of this bias after it was announced that she was in the first group of women selected to be an artillery officer in the Marine Corps:

> There was a lot of negativity that I didn't expect. Everyone was really supportive when they knew I wanted Artillery but they didn't think it would actually happen. As soon as it happened, there was this "Oh, man, they're actually coming" feeling. There was this one guy in my platoon who was one of my closest friends, and as soon as I got Artillery he just completely cut ties and didn't speak with me at all. I thought, wow, that's harsh. So eventually I pulled him aside and asked him what's going on. He said, "I just don't want women here, but I believe in you and I want you to succeed. It's just going to take a little time for me to get used to that." This was something I didn't expect to happen.

At least Virginia Brodie's peer was self-aware enough to understand how he was feeling. A half a century ago, many of us might have told a woman aspiring to lead, "Now, don't you worry your pretty little head about it." Today, benevolent sexism may be more subtle, for instance, when a candidate list for a prime leadership job is generated, all the names are male. Worse, mentors to women never stop to ask why.

Gentlemen, beware those ostensibly benevolent, superficially posi-tive thoughts and comments about women that convey an undertone of dismissal and that reinforce stereotypes about female dependence upon men. Make this a general practice in the workplace, but be especially vigilant in your mentoring relationships with women. And if you catch yourself making a sexist remark—no matter how benign—fess up, apol-ogize, and vow to do better. We predict she'll appreciate your sincerity.

44. No Cloning Allowed!

Gentlemen, beware the temptation to clone yourself in your mentees.

In a classic research study from the world of academe, exceptionally prolific college professors were asked to nominate their "most success-ful protégés."[9] When the researchers then studied the careers of these favored mentees, they discovered stunning similarities between mentors and mentees in terms of career choices and trajectory. In many ways, these "most successful" mentees had followed career paths that mirrored their mentors'.

Gentlemen, be sober and concerned about the deep-seated—often entirely unconscious—desire to validate your own life choices and career decisions through your mentees. It can feel profoundly gratifying when a mentee who admires and respects you decides to follow in your footsteps. It can be a tantalizing stroke to the ego when a woman you mentor replicates key portions of your own professional and life journey. We are all at risk of becoming enamored with and showing favoritism to mentees who validate our career decisions by making the same deci-sions. After all, imitation truly is the highest form of flattery.

Perhaps the most dangerous aspect of the tendency to clone ourselves in the women we mentor is the fact that the motivation to do so oper-ates below the radar of consciousness. If asked, most of us would give loud support for the virtue of encouraging a mentee to follow her own path, but in practice, we too often advise, cajole, pressure, and some-times flat-out insist that mentees follow in our own footsteps.[10] Consider this warning about cloning from Dr. Nadine Kaslow of Emory Uni-versity's School of Medicine: "It is imperative not to mentor people to be just like you! People thrive when mentored to be their own person.

I think many women are particularly sensitive to the messaging about what you're supposed to be like. So when mentoring women, you've got to go out of your way to let them follow their own path and pursue their own interests. This was one of the most significant things my male mentors did for me."

Here are some of the most negative side effects that can accrue when a man endeavors to replicate himself in his female mentee:

◆ *Distress*: Imposing his own model of a successful career onto a mentee can create significant stress and anxiety in a woman.[11] This may be compounded if she has been socialized to please and comply in order to guarantee support and affirmation.

◆ *Suppression of her dreams and aspirations*: A mentor set on cloning himself in a mentee will often be blind to her unique vision of success, her priorities, and the developmental needs he should be attending to in an effort to get her there.

◆ *Exacerbation of work–life conflicts*: Because men have less often been required to share equally in child-rearing and household duties, unconscious cloning can make him insensitive to her work–life priorities. For instance, such a mentor might suggest to a female mentee that she forgo or delay having children in order to devote more time to her career. This might easily result in a painful bind in which she feels compelled to choose between a successful career and her desire for a family.[12]

◆ *Diminished mentoring*: A mentor may lose interest in a mentee who wishes to chart her own career path and take a route less familiar to the mentor. His engagement with her development and the value of the relationship may dim slowly, leaving her confused or perhaps convinced she has become a disappointment.

◆ *Resentment*: Although she may crave acceptance and affirmation from her mentor—as most mentees do—a mentee may become resentful and ambivalent about the mentorship when the mentor's expectations and demands for her to copy his example become an unwanted burden.

Gentlemen, beware the thin boundary between career coaching and cloning. Accept that you are likely to be most attracted to mentoring women and men who most remind you of yourself. Recognize that the process of creating an affirming mirror image of yourself in a mentee is often insidious and unconscious. Discuss the risk of cloning openly with each mentee and ask her to bring it to your attention immediately should she feel coerced or pressured to deviate from her career dream in order to please you.

45. Never Entertain the Possibility of Sex

Guys, let's get real. If you are heterosexual and if you mentor women often, it is exceptionally likely that you may find some of those women attractive, emotionally and physically. And you won't be alone. Your trusted authors would be lying if we told you we'd never been aware of feeling some measure of attraction to a rising Athena now and then. But let's get right to the punch line of element 45: no amount of attraction, bonding, or emotional intimacy EVER gives you clearance to sexualize a relationship with a woman you mentor, particularly when you hold any sort of power relative to her. Men, this is a bright-line boundary. No exceptions. Deal with it.

All right, with that out of the way, let's talk about why sexual feelings are not at all unusual or shameful when mentoring across sex. We'll also discuss how to think about these feelings and, most important, what to do with them.

Many strong cross-sex mentoring relationships conjure a delightful sense of excitement, synergy, creative exchange, and increasing levels of mutuality and intimacy, often between a man and a woman who share salient career aspirations, professional interests, and values.[13] Moreover, the mentoring pair may enjoy close proximity, frequent interaction, and sometimes intense work together. As mentor and mentee discover slowly increasing and mutual affection, respect, trust, self-disclosure, and a sense of closeness, it should come as absolutely no surprise to anyone if feelings of attraction and erotic tension enter the mentorship equation at times.[14] Although some measure of mutual liking and attraction are actually quite enjoyable, synergistic, and motivating, the value of a mentorship is placed in peril when one or both members of the relationship wish to add a sexual liaison.[15] Erotic attraction can lead to either violation of important relationship boundaries or anxiety that ultimately provokes distancing and withdrawal from what was heretofore a valuable developmental relationship.

Gentlemen, a few of your closest and most meaningful mentorships with women might approach what psychologist Robert Sternberg would call *companionate love*. According to Sternberg's *triangular theory of love*,[16] when relationships include two key ingredients, they describe strong sibling connections, close personal friendships, and many enduring and particularly strong mentorships. These ingredients are: (1) *intimacy*, which encourages feelings of closeness, connectedness, and bondedness, and (2) *commitment*, which encompasses the decision to stick together, providing support and backing even when the going gets rough. In their interviews with women about their high-impact mentorships with men, researchers Joan Jeruchim and Pat Shapiro found an undertone of companionate love: "Many women told us that they loved their mentors. This was not a sexual love but an intense emotional attachment."[17]

Guys, although there is nothing inherently wrong with some emotional intimacy and commitment in a mentorship—in fact, these are two elements most likely to lead to good work together in the long term things get dicey when the third component of love relationships, *passion*, makes its appearance. According to Sternberg, passion encompasses the drives that lead to romance, physical attraction, and sexual consummation.[18] Let us be frank, gentlemen: a sexually intimate relationship with a mentee is nearly always destructive (personally and professionally) and ultimately painful for the mentee, not to mention disruptive to the workplace and toxic to your own reputation and career.[19] Any sexual behavior between a man who holds power and a woman he mentors is inherently exploitive of a woman's trust and an unequivocal violation of professional boundaries.[20] It is inherently confusing to a mentee who can no longer be sure how to think about her relationship to her mentor. Despite all the warnings men routinely hear about honoring fiduciary responsibilities to women they mentor, women continue to experience sexual advances and other boundary violations from men they counted on for mentorship.

Men, there are some ever-present risk factors for romanticized and sexualized mentorships with women. Know them, let them heighten your self-awareness, and be sober about their capacity to nudge you onto that slippery slope toward boundary violations with your mentee.[21] We offer them here in no particular order:

* *Your life circumstances*: Men experiencing marriage problems, divorce, midlife adjustment issues, career stagnation, loneliness, doubts about their own attractiveness, and hidden depression are at greater risk of sexualizing a mentorship.

* *Your own psychological needs*: Men with strong dependency or narcissistic needs may have a powerful drive to be validated, affirmed, and cared for in an intimate workplace relationship with a woman.

* *Being admired and needed*: Men who discover powerful gratification in a relationship with a woman who admires, idealizes, and needs them may find the notion of sexual union so alluring that all the bright-line prohibitions against sex in a professional relationship become hazy and distant.

* *Power as an aphrodisiac*: Men who hold positions of significant power and prestige are often seen as more attractive to the women they mentor; power dynamics can easily become entwined with sexual dynamics.

* *Kindness and support as an aphrodisiac*: Men who are supportive, encouraging, and engaged with women when the rest of the organizational culture is hostile and unsupportive may elicit stronger attachment and emotional or physical enmeshment from women who feel isolated at work.

* *Emotional vulnerability in a woman*: Women with low self-esteem, a strong need for approval from an authority figure, or a history of

exploitation by previous men in their lives may be more vulnerable to blurring boundaries in a mentoring relationship.

All right, gentlemen, we've established that romantic and sexual feelings can evolve around the periphery of an otherwise healthy and productive mentorship with a woman. We've determined that this has happened from time to time for nearly every guy who cares enough to intentionally mentor women. It *does not* mean you are creepy, weak, or abnormal. And, we've agreed that there are certain red flags and risk factors for sexualizing a mentorship that demand your careful attention and ongoing self-awareness. Finally, we've established that it is your sworn duty to manage these feelings appropriately and prevent them from turning a strong mentorship into something else, possibly exploiting your mentee and diminishing her career along the way. To make your task a bit easier, here are some final recommendations for keeping your mentorships with women on the up and up. We encourage you to take them in and review them from time to time.[22]

♦ Remain aware of your own needs for affirmation and intimacy from women; be deliberate about getting these needs met outside of your mentorships.

♦ When your own emotional health or marriage is at low ebb, when you feel particularly lonely, or as the middle phase of life and career approaches, be particularly vigilant to boundaries in your mentorships.

♦ Remind yourself that intimacy and attraction to a mentee can magnify fantasies that she is a "perfect match," when in fact you know comparatively little about her.

♦ When attraction and romantic thoughts threaten to derail a mentorship, tighten up your boundaries, make the mentorship even more public and transparent (watch those closed-door meetings), and remind yourself over and over again just how destructive a sexualized mentorship is likely to be for her *and* for you!

◆ Do NOT share feelings of attraction or romantic fantasies with your mentee. This is an unfair burden to put on her and it may paradoxically serve only to heighten intimacy. DO disclose your feelings to a trusted colleague (male or female)—possibly someone external to the organization—so that a reliable and confidential peer can help you with accountability and reality testing.

◆ If all else fails, give yourself a brisk slap to the face, or ask a really big guy to kick you hard in the nuts. Better that than the calamity you can inflict on your mentee and upon yourself should you fail to honor your ethical responsibility to do no harm.

46. Never Attempt to Hide the Mentorship from Your Spouse or Partner

Gentlemen, in this final element, we conclude this guide for male mentors with a word of admonition about your marriage or partnership. It is never a good idea to keep an important mentoring relationship secret from your significant other.

In some of the pioneering studies of cross-sex mentorships, concerns about the jealous spouse were among the more frequent reasons that men were reluctant to mentor women.[23] Wives of mentors were often quite resistant to the idea of their husband having a close relationship with a member of the opposite sex, especially if the two occasionally traveled together for work. To some extent, the same concerns and necessary caution hold true today. If your partner is prone to jealousy, or if things are rocky in your relationship, she might be especially sensitive to your devotion of time and commitment to another woman at work, especially if that mentee is younger and attractive. Remember our lesson on human evolution; on a primal level, this "other woman" could be seen as a direct threat to your partner's well-being.

Guys, the potential for spousal or partner jealousy is not a reasonable excuse to avoid mentoring women. You've just got to be thoughtful, deliberate, and transparent when you do. And for goodness' sake, don't ever make the mistake of keeping a significant or ongoing mentorship with a woman secret from your partner. If she is already sensitive and a bit prone to jealousy, imagine how she'll feel at that holiday party when your mentee introduces herself and proclaims her appreciation for all the time and assistance you've provided...Not good. And why would you want to threaten the health and happiness of a marriage or committed relationship by hiding a mentorship? Several of the women we spoke to when preparing this guide mentioned their concern for their mentor's spouse.

When Becky Halstead, Army Brigadier General (ret), served as personal aide to an Army general, she decided to be proactive in thwarting any misperception or jealousy on the part of his spouse: "The way I dealt with the challenge was to do my very best to nurture a relationship with his spouse. I wanted her to know who I was as a person and an officer. I was always very careful to be approachable, respectful, and to make sure that there were never any hidden conversations. Those of us who are being mentored by a man need to respect that and not ignore the feelings of spouses."

And, let's not forget to think about the mentee's spouse, gentlemen. How might he feel if his spouse raves about you all the time? Dr. Susan Madsen described her approach to bringing her spouse into her relationships with important male mentors over the years: "My husband has always been so supportive. I talked about my mentors a lot because that was so important in my career and what was happening at the moment. My husband really enjoyed hearing about it and, in fact, he got to know all three of my mentors well. I think it was important for him to know them because they were important people in my life."

We think Becky Halstead and Susan Madsen are excellent role models for our primary recommendation for managing potential misunderstanding or jealousy on the part of your partner: do *not* attempt to hide any of your mentorships from her! Why would you? It is the twenty-first century; men have got to mentor women and mentor them deliberately. If your partner is so intensely jealous that she cannot tolerate the idea of you interacting with and championing the careers of women at work, it may be time for couples therapy or serious reconsideration of the health of your relationship.

At the same time, a spouse's jealousy is sometimes just the wake-up call you need. Has a mentorship with a woman begun to veer into dangerous territory? Are you becoming sneaky, having clandestine meetings or conversations with your mentee? Are you hiding the relationship from your spouse and coworkers? Then it's time to reread element 45 and check yourself and your feelings of attraction.

If your otherwise calm and supportive partner is sounding an alarm, she might just be saving you from a colossal blunder.

PARTING THOUGHTS

We applaud your commitment to reading a whole book on mentoring women. Clearly you have the right stuff to take on the "that guy" mantle in the workplace. Be comfortable in your own skin. Recognize and own the biology and psychology of your male architecture. Work to better understand and appreciate the women around you. Accept that your own maleness can at times facilitate or impede effective mentorships. Be an intentional and deliberate mentor for women. Remain vigilant for those everyday Athenas; push them forward and watch them soar.

Mentoring women well is what good men do. Take the elements in this book to heart, practice them daily, in the crucible of your own workplace and in full view of your colleagues. Stay out front and mentor women without being asked. Do these things and you'll contribute to your organization's bottom line, you'll bolster the career success and the spirit of the women you mentor, and for all of this, you'll be a better man. For your good work, we thank you in advance.

Onward!

ACKNOWLEDGMENTS

This book would not have come to fruition without the enthusiastic and steadfast support of several key women. First, our wives, Laura and Erica daily embody love, character, and partnership in the finest sense of those words. Second, twenty high-flying women who have advanced to the top tiers of leadership in a range of professions and organizations graciously allowed us to interview them in preparation for writing this guide. Their wisdom, wit, and perspective on the vicissitudes of cross-gender mentorships imbued our writing with the authority and real-life texture born of their hard-earned experience. Third, Catalyst's Deborah Gillis and Julie Nugent were instrumental in providing resources and access throughout our research and writing. Fourth, we are ever-indebted to our literary agent, Carol Mann. Carol instantly saw promise in our idea and has championed our work at every turn. Finally, the brilliant, creative, and encouraging women of Bibliomotion, Inc. have made the book publishing odyssey a delight from start to finish. We are especially grateful to Erika Heilman, Jill Friedlander, Shevaun Betzler, Ari Choquette, Susan Lauzau, Erin Leddy, Jill Schoenhaut, and Alicia Simons. Thank you ladies!

NOTES

Preface

1. Alissa Greenberg, "A Nobel Scientist Just Made a Breathtakingly Sexist Speech at International Conference," *Time*, June 10, 2015, accessed April 14, 2016, http://time.com/3915617/women-science-tim-hunt-nobel-sexist/.
2. Sarah Mimms, "Why Some Male Members of Congress Won't Be Alone with Female Staffers," *Atlantic*, May 14, 2015, accessed April 14, 2016, https://www.nationaljournal.com/s/27043/why-some-male-members-congress-wont-be-alone-with-female-staffers.
3. Hope Hodge Seck, "Controversy Surrounds Firing of Marines' Female Recruit Battalion CO," *Marine Corps Times*, July 15, 2015, accessed April 14, 2016, http://www.marinecorpstimes.com/story/military/2015/07/07/kate-germano-fired-marine-corps-female-recruit-unit-commander/29763371/.
4. W. Brad Johnson and Charles R. Ridley, *The Elements of Mentoring*.

Chapter 1

1. John Gerzema and Michael D'Antonio, *The Athena Doctrine*, 256.
2. Howard Fullerton, "Labor Force Participation," 3; U.S. Bureau of Labor Statistics, "Women in the Labor Force."
3. Michelle Budig and Paula England, "The Wage Penalty for Motherhood," 204–05; Shelley Correll, Stephen Benard, and In Paik, "Getting a Job: Is There a Motherhood Penalty?," 1297.
4. Madeline E. Heilman and Michelle C. Haynes, "No Credit Where Credit Is Due: Attributional Rationalization of Women's Success in Male–Female Teams," 905.

5. Mark Lutter, "Do Women Suffer from Network Closure?," 346.
6. Ibid.
7. Ibid.
8. Ibid.
9. Ibid.
10. Anna Fels, "Do Women Lack Ambition?," 52.
11. "Women in the Workplace."
12. Ibid.
13. Ibid.
14. "Implementation of the Full Integration of Women in the Armed Forces"; "Department of the Navy Talent Management Initiatives."

Chapter 2

1. Steffen Andersen, Seda Ertac, Uri Gneezy, John A. List, and Sandra Maximiano, "Gender, Competitiveness, and Socialization at a Young Age," 1438.
2. Alison Booth and Patrick Nolen, "Choosing to Compete," 542.
3. Joan C. Williams and Rachel Dempsey, *What Works for Women at Work*.
4. M. Ena Inesi and Daniel M. Cable, "When Accomplishments Come Back to Haunt You," 615.
5. Madeline E. Heilman and Michelle C. Haynes, "No Credit Where Credit Is Due: Attributional Rationalization of Women's Success in Male–Female Teams," 905.
6. Rachel Croson and Uri Gneezy, "Gender Differences in Preferences," 448.
7. Wendy Wang, Kim C. Parker, and Paul Taylor, *Breadwinner Moms*.
8. Kim Parker, *5 Facts About Today's Fathers*.
9. Christopher D. DeSante, "Working Twice As Hard to Get Half As Far," 342.
10. Jennifer L. Berdahl and Celia Moore, "Workplace Harassment: Double Jeopardy for Minority Women," 426.
11. Dana Kabat-Farr and Lilia M. Cortina, "Selective Incivility," 120.
12. Alice H. Eagly and Linda L. Carli, *Through the Labyrinth*; Debra Meyerson, *Tempered Radicals*, xi.
13. Steven J. Spencer, Claude M. Steele, and Diane M. Quinn, "Stereotype Threat and Women's Math Performance," 4.
14. Ibid.
15. Paul G. Davies, Steven J. Spencer, and Claude M. Steele, "Clearing the Air," 276.
16. Crystal L. Hoyt and Jim Blascovich, "Leadership Efficacy and Women Leaders' Responses to Stereotype Activation," 595.

Chapter 3

1. Sylvia Ann Hewlett, Kerrie Peraino, Laura Sherbin, and Karen Sumberg, *The Sponsor Effect.*
2. Sheryl Sandberg, *Lean In.*
3. Claudia Goldin and Cecilia Rouse, "Orchestrating Impartiality," 715.
4. Alice H. Eagly and Steven J. Karau, "Role Congruity Theory of Prejudice Toward Female Leaders," 573; Chieh-Chen Bowen, Janet K. Swim, and Rick R. Jacobs, "Evaluating Gender Biases on Actual Job Performance of Real People," 2194.
5. Katherine L. Milkman, Modupe Akinola, and Dolly Chugh, "What Happens Before," 1678.
6. Kristen Jones, Kathy Stewart, Eden King, Whitney Botsford Morgan, Veronica Gilrane, and Kimberly Hylton, "Negative Consequence of Benevolent Sexism on Efficacy and Performance," 189.
7. Sarah Mimms, "Why Some Male Members of Congress Won't Be Alone with Female Staffers."
8. Sandberg, *Lean In.*
9. Sylvia Ann Hewlett, Kerrie Peraino, Laura Sherbin, and Karen Sumberg, *The Sponsor Effect.*
10. Kim Elsesser, *Sex and the Office.*
11. Herminia Ibarra, Nancy M. Carter, and Christine Silva, "Why Men Still Get More Promotions Than Women," 80.

Chapter 4

1. "Mars vs. Venus: The Gender Gap in Health," *Harvard Men's Health Watch.*
2. Ibid.
3. Daphna Joel, Zohar Berman, Ido Tavor, Nadav Wexler, Olga Gaber, Yaniv Stein, Nisan Shefi et al., "Sex Beyond the Genitalia," 15468.
4. Ibid.
5. Turhan Canli, John E. Desmond, Zuo Zhao, and John D. Gabrieli, "Sex Differences in the Neural Basis of Emotional Memories," 10789; Jacob Miguel Vigil, "A Socio-Relational Framework of Sex Differences in the Expression of Emotion," 375; Sarah Whittle, Murat Yücel, Marie B. Yap, and Nicholas B. Allen, "Sex Differences in the Neural Correlates of Emotion," 319.
6. Diane F. Halpern, *Sex Differences in Cognitive Abilities.*
7. Thomas Buser and Noemi Peter, "Multitasking," 641.

8. Shira Offer and Barbara Schneider, "Revisiting the Gender Gap in Time-Use Patterns Multitasking and Well-Being Among Mothers and Fathers in Dual-Earner Families," 809.

9. Kateri McRae, Kevin N. Ochsner, Iris B. Mauss, John J. Gabrieli, and James J. Gross, "Gender Differences in Emotion Regulation," 143.

10. Ibid.

11. Ibid.

12. Dianne A. van Hemert, Fons J. van de Vijver, and Ad J. Vingerhoets, "Culture and Crying Prevalences and Gender Differences," 399.

13. Karl Grammer, Bernhard Fink, and Nick Neave, "Human Pheromones and Sexual Attraction," 135; Anastasia Makhanova and Saul L. Miller, "Female Fertility and Male Mating," 389; Jon K. Maner and James K. McNulty, "Attunement to the Fertility Status of Same-Sex Rivals," 412.

14. Devendra Singh, Barbara J. Dixson, Thomas S. Jessop, Bethan Morgan, and Alan F. Dixson, "Cross-Cultural Consensus for Waist–Hip Ratio and Women's Attractiveness," 176.

15. David M. Buss, "The Great Struggles of Life," 140.

16. Jean-Yves Baudouin and Guy Tiberghien, "Symmetry, Averageness, and Feature Size in the Facial Attractiveness of Women," 313; Karl Grammer and Randy Thornhill, "Human (Homo sapiens) Facial Attractiveness and Sexual Selection," 233. Devendra Singh, Barbara J. Dixson, Thomas S. Jessop, Bethan Morgan, and Alan F. Dixson, "Cross-Cultural Consensus for Waist–Hip Ratio and Women's Attractiveness," 180.

17. Sarah J. Gervais, Theresa K. Vescio, Jens Förster, Anne Maass, and Caterina Suitner, "Seeing Women As Objects," 743.

18. April Bleske-Rechek, Erin Somers, Cierra Micke, Leah Erickson, Lindsay Matteson, Corey Stocco, Brittany Schumacher, and Laura Ritchie, "Benefit or Burden? Attraction in Cross-Sex Friendship," 569.

19. Ibid.

20. Joseph H. Pleck, *The Myth of Masculinity*.

21. Candace West and Don H. Zimmerman, "Doing Gender," 125.

22. Pleck, *The Myth of Masculinity*; West and Zimmerman, "Doing Gender."

23. Sonja Feist-Price, "Cross-Gender Mentoring Relationships," 13; Rosabeth Moss Kanter, *Men and Women of the Corporation*.

24. Feist-Price, "Cross-Gender Mentoring Relationships," 13; Kanter, *Men and Women of the Corporation*.

25. Ibid.

Chapter 5

1. Belle Rose Ragins and John L. Cotton, "Mentor Functions and Outcomes," 529; Belle Rose Ragins and Kathy E. Kram, *The Handbook of Mentoring at Work: Theory, Research, and Practice.*
2. Lind-Eling Lee, Ric Marshall, Damion Rallis, and Matt Moscardi, "Women on Boards"; Hanna Rosin, *The End of Men*; Siri Terjesen, Ruth Sealy, and Val Singh, "Women Directors on Corporate Boards," 320.
3. Ronald J. Burke and Eddy Ng, "The Changing Nature of Work and Organizations," 86.
4. Burke and Ng, "The Changing Nature of Work and Organizations," 86; Alice H. Eagly and Jean Lau Chin, "Diversity and Leadership in a Changing World," 216; Rosin, *The End of Men.*
5. Barbara Annis and John Gray, *Work with Me.*
6. Pamela J. Kalbfleisch and Joann Keyton, "Power and Equality in Mentoring Relationships," 189; Sheryl Sandberg, *Lean In.*
7. Ragins and Kram, *The Handbook of Mentoring at Work: Theory, Research, and Practice.*
8. Sylvia Beyer, "Gender Differences in the Accuracy of Self-Evaluations of Performance," 960.
9. Madeline E. Heilman and Michelle C. Haynes, "No Credit Where Credit Is Due: Attributional Rationalization of Women's Success in Male–Female Teams," 905.
10. Tara Mohr, "Why Women Don't Apply for Jobs Unless They're 100% Qualified"; Joan C. Williams and Rachel Dempsey, *What Works for Women at Work.*
11. Carol Dweck, *Mindset*; Kray, Laura J. Kray, and Michael P. Haselhuhn, "Male Pragmatism in Negotiators' Ethical Reasoning," 1124; Raef A. Lawson, "Is Classroom Cheating Related to Business Students' Propensity to Cheat in the 'Real World'?," 189.
12. Kram, "Improving the Mentoring Process."
13. Kathryn Taaffe McLearn, Diane Colasanto, and Cathy Schoen, *Mentoring Makes a Difference.*
14. W. Brad Johnson, *On Being a Mentor.*
15. Katy Dickinson, Tanya Jankot, and Helen Gracon, "Sun Mentoring: 1996–2009."
16. Johnson, *On Being a Mentor.*
17. Sandberg, *Lean In.*
18. Kent Keith, *Anyway: The Paradoxical Commandments: Finding Personal Meaning in a Crazy World.*

19. Daniel A. Effron and Dale T. Miller, "How the Moralization of Issues Grants Social Legitimacy to Act on One's Attitudes," 690.

Chapter 6

1. Belle Rose Ragins and John L. Cotton, "Mentor Functions and Outcomes," 529.
2. Pamela J. Kalbfleisch and Joann Keyton, "Power and Equality in Mentoring Relationships," 189.
3. Kathy E. Kram, "Improving the Mentoring Process."
4. Pamela J. Kalbfleisch, "Appeasing the Mentor," 389.
5. Sandy Jeanquart-Barone and Uma Sekaran, "Effects of Supervisor's Gender on American Women's Trust," 253.
6. Dana L. Haggard and Daniel B. Turban, "The Mentoring Relationship As a Context for Psychological Contract Development," 1904.
7. Peter Rutter, *Sex in the Forbidden Zone.*
8. Lois A. Benishek, Kathleen J. Bieschke, Jeeseon Park, and Suzanne M. Slattery, "A Multicultural Feminist Model of Mentoring," 428.
9. George F. Dreher and Ronald A. Ash, "A Comparative Study of Mentoring Among Men and Women in Managerial, Professional, and Technical Positions," 539; Catherine A. Hansman, "Mentoring and Women's Career Development," 63.
10. Sherry L. Harden, Richard A. Clark, W. Brad Johnson, and Joshua Larson, "Cross-Gender Mentorship in Clinical Psychology Doctoral Programs," 277; Committee on Maximizing the Potential of Women in Academic Science and Engineering, National Academy of Sciences, National Academy of Engineering, and Institute of Medicine, *Biological, Social, and Organizational Components of Success for Women in Academic Science and Engineering*; Raymond A. Noe, "An Investigation of the Determinants of Successful Assigned Mentoring Relationships," 457.
11. Alice H. Eagly and Jean Lau Chin, "Diversity and Leadership in a Changing World," 216.
12. Anna Fels, "Do Women Lack Ambition?," 50.
13. Henry Etzkowitz, Carol Kemelgor, and Brian Uzzi, *Athena Unbound*; Rayona Sharpnack, "What Do Men Get Out of Advancing Women?"
14. Kathy E. Kram, "Improving the Mentoring Process."
15. Amy E. Hurley, "Challenges in Cross-Gender Mentoring Relationships," 42.
16. Joan Jeruchim and Patricia Gottlieb Shapiro, *Women, Mentors, and Success*; Kram, "Improving the Mentoring Process."

17. Lucia A. Gilbert, "Female and Male Emotional Dependency and Its Implications for the Therapist–Client Relationship," 555; Kram, "Improving the Mentoring Process"; S. Michael Plaut, "Boundary Issues in Teacher–Student Relationships," 210; Joseph H. Pleck, *The Myth of Masculinity.*

18. Kram, "Improving the Mentoring Process."

19. John Gerzema and Michael D'Antonio, *The Athena Doctrine*; Sharpnack, "What Do Men Get Out of Advancing Women?"

20. Sheryl Sandberg, *Lean In.*

21. Adam Grant, "Why So Many Men Don't Stand Up for Their Female Colleagues"; Jeanine Prime, Mike Otterman, and Elizabeth R. Salib, "Engaging Men Through Inclusive Leadership," 385.

22. Grant, "Why So Many Men Don't Stand Up for Their Female Colleagues."

23. Catherine A. Hansman, "Mentoring and Women's Career Development," 63; Margaret M. Hopkins, Deborah A. O'Neil, Angela Passarelli, and Diana Bilimoria, "Women's Leadership Development Strategic Practices for Women and Organizations," 348; Pamela J. Kalbfleisch and Joann Keyton, "Power and Equality in Mentoring Relationships," 189; Kram, "Improving the Mentoring Process."

24. Joshua N. Hook, Don E. Davis, Jesse Owen, Everett L. Worthington Jr, and Shawn O. Utsey, "Cultural Humility," 353.

25. Wendy Wood and Alice H. Eagly, "A Cross-Cultural Analysis of the Behavior of Women and Men," 699.

26. Jeruchim and Shapiro, *Women, Mentors, and Success.*

27. Ronald J. Burke and Carol A. McKeen, "Gender Effects in Mentoring Relationships," 91; Terri A. Scandura and Ethlyn A. Williams, "An Investigation of the Moderating Effects of Gender on the Relationships Between Mentorship Initiation and Protégé Perceptions of Mentoring Functions," 342.

28. McKeen and Burke, 1989; Noe, 1988.

29. Sandberg, *Lean In*, 65.

30. McKeen and Burke, "Mentor Relationships in Organisations," 33.

31. Sandberg, *Lean In*, 72.

32. Sharpnack, "What Do Men Get Out of Advancing Women?"

Chapter 7

1. Jason Headley, "It's Not About the Nail."

2. Lucia A. Gilbert and Karen M. Rossman, "Gender and the Mentoring Process for Women," 233.

3. Catherine Elliott, Joanne D. Leck, Barbara Orser, and Catherine Mossop, "An Exploration of Gender and Trust in Mentoring Relationships," 1; Belle Liang, Allison J. Tracy, Catherine A. Taylor, and Linda M. Williams, "Mentoring College-Age Women: A Relational Approach," 271.
4. Tammy D. Allen, "Mentoring Others," 134; Carl R. Rogers, "The Necessary and Sufficient Conditions of Therapeutic Personality Change," 95.
5. Lois A. Benishek, Kathleen J. Bieschke, Jeeseon Park, and Suzanne M. Slattery, "A Multicultural Feminist Model of Mentoring," 428; Kathy E. Kram, "Improving the Mentoring Process"; Carol A. McKeen and Ronald J. Burke, "Mentor Relationships in Organisations," 33.
6. Belle Rose Ragins, "Relational Mentoring," 519.
7. Ragins, "Relational Mentoring," 531.
8. Liang et al., "Mentoring College-Age Women: A Relational Approach," 271.
9. Sherry L. Harden, Richard A. Clark, W. Brad Johnson, and Joshua Larson, "Cross-Gender Mentorship in Clinical Psychology Doctoral Programs," 277; Liang et al., "Mentoring College-Age Women: A Relational Approach," 271.
10. Amy E. Hurley, "Challenges in Cross-Gender Mentoring Relationships," 42; Harden et al., "Cross-Gender Mentorship in Clinical Psychology Doctoral Programs," 277.
11. Shelley E. Taylor, *The Tending Instinct.*
12. Rogers, "The Necessary and Sufficient Conditions of Therapeutic Personality Change," 95.
13. Ibid.
14. Joan Jeruchim and Patricia Gottlieb Shapiro, *Women, Mentors, and Success*; Sheryl Sandberg, *Lean In.*
15. Amy Aldridge Sanford, Elaina M. Ross, Shawna J. Blake, and Renée L. Cambiano, "Finding Courage and Confirmation," 31.
16. Michael Johns, Toni Schmader, and Andy Martens, "Knowing Is Half the Battle: Teaching Stereotype Threat As a Means of Improving Women's Math Performance," 175.
17. Henry Etzkowitz, Carol Kemelgor, and Brian Uzzi, *Athena Unbound.*
18. Naomi C. Chesler and Mark A. Chesler, "Gender-Informed Mentoring Strategies for Women Engineering Scholars," 49.
19. Lois A. Benishek, Kathleen J. Bieschke, Jeeseon Park, and Suzanne M. Slattery, "A Multicultural Feminist Model of Mentoring," 428; Harden et al., "Cross-Gender Mentorship in Clinical Psychology Doctoral Programs," 277.
20. W. Brad Johnson, *On Being a Mentor*; Carol A. Mullen, *Mentorship Primer.*
21. Johnson, *On Being a Mentor.*

22. Jeanine Prime, Mike Otterman, and Elizabeth R. Salib, "Engaging Men Through Inclusive Leadership," 385; Belle Rose Ragins and John L. Cotton, "Mentor Functions and Outcomes," 529; Ragins and Dean B. McFarlin, "Perceptions of Mentor Roles in Cross-Gender Mentoring Relationships," 321.

23. Catherine Elliott, Joanne D. Leck, Barbara Orser, and Catherine Mossop, "An Exploration of Gender and Trust in Mentoring Relationships," 1; Hurley, "Challenges in Cross-Gender Mentoring Relationships," 42.

24. Kram, "Improving the Mentoring Process."

25. Hurley, "Challenges in Cross-Gender Mentoring Relationships," 42; Kram, "Improving the Mentoring Process."

26. James G. Clawson and Kathy E. Kram, "Managing Cross-Gender Mentoring," 22.

27. Kram, "Improving the Mentoring Process."

28. Clawson and Kram, "Managing Cross-Gender Mentoring," 22.

29. Sandberg, *Lean In.*

30. Scott A. Myers, Gregory A. Cranmer, Zachary W. Goldman, Michael Sollitto, Hailey G. Gillen, and Hannah Ball, "Differences in Information Seeking Among Organizational Peers: Perceptions of Appropriateness, Importance, and Frequency."

31. Clawson and Kram, "Managing Cross-Gender Mentoring," 22.

32. Johnson, *On Being a Mentor.*

33. Jeruchim and Shapiro, *Women, Mentors, and Success.*

34. Monica C. Higgins, Dawn E. Chandler, and Kathy E. Kram, "Developmental Initiation and Developmental Networks," 349.

35. Johnson, *On Being a Mentor*; W. Brad Johnson and Charles R. Ridley, *The Elements of Mentoring.*

36. Liang et al., "Mentoring College-Age Women: A Relational Approach," 271.

Chapter 8

1. Henry Etzkowitz, Carol Kemelgor, and Brian Uzzi, *Athena Unbound.*

2. Lawton Wehle Fitt and Derek A. Newton, "When the Mentor Is a Man and the Protege a Woman," 56.

3. Etzkowitz et al., *Athena Unbound.*

4. Peggy Drexler, "Why You Need to Brag More (And How to Do It)."

5. W. Brad Johnson, *On Being a Mentor.*

6. Lori L. Davis, Marc S. Little, and William L. Thornton, "The Art and Angst of the Mentoring Relationship," 61.

7. W. Brad Johnson and Charles R. Ridley, *The Elements of Mentoring*; Naomi C. Chesler and Mark A. Chesler, "Gender-Informed Mentoring Strategies for Women Engineering Scholars: On Establishing a Caring Community, 49.

8. Sheryl Sandberg, *Lean In*.

9. Belle Rose Ragins, "Relational Mentoring," 519.

10. Johnson and Ridley, *The Elements of Mentoring*; Kathy E. Kram, "Improving the Mentoring Process."

11. Ellen A. Ensher and Susan E. Murphy, "The Mentoring Relationship Challenges Scale," 253.

12. Ibid.

13. Etzkowitz et al., *Athena Unbound*.

14. Chesler and Chesler, "Gender-Informed Mentoring Strategies for Women Engineering Scholars," 49; Johnson, *On Being a Mentor*.

15. Johnson and Ridley, *The Elements of Mentoring*.

16. Kram, "Improving the Mentoring Process."

17. Herminia Ibarra, Nancy M. Carter, and Christine Silva, "Why Men Still Get More Promotions Than Women," 80.

18. Johnson and Ridley, *The Elements of Mentoring*.

19. Ellen A. Fagenson, "The Power of a Mentor: Protégés' and Nonprotégés' Perceptions of Their Own Power in Organizations," 182; Lawton Wehle Fitt and Derek A. Newton, "When the Mentor Is a Man and the Protege a Woman," 56; Lucia A. Gilbert and Karen M. Rossman, "Gender and the Mentoring Process for Women: Implications for Professional Development," 233.

20. Johnson and Ridley, *The Elements of Mentoring*.

21. Harriet Zuckerman, *Scientific Elite*; Christine Charyton, John O. Elliott, Mohammed A. Rahman, Jeness L. Woodard, and Samantha DeDios, "Gender and Science," 203.

22. Alice H. Eagly and Jean Lau Chin, "Diversity and Leadership in a Changing World," 216; Hanna Rosin, *The End of Men*.

23. Ronald J. Burke and Eddy Ng, "The Changing Nature of Work and Organizations," 86.

24. Rosin, *The End of Men*.

25. Alice H. Eagly and Linda L. Carli, *Through the Labyrinth*; Eagly and Blair T. Johnson, "Gender and Leadership Style," 233; Margaret M. Hopkins, Deborah A. O'Neil, Angela Passarelli, and Diana Bilimoria, "Women's Leadership Development: Strategic Practices for Women and Organizations," 348.

26. John Gerzema and Michael D'Antonio, *The Athena Doctrine*.

27. S. Nierenberg and C. Marvin, "Women 'Take Care,' Men 'Take Charge'"; Eagly

and Carli, *Through the Labyrinth*; Eagly and Chin, "Diversity and Leadership in a Changing World."

28. Eagly and Chin, "Diversity and Leadership in a Changing World."
29. Thomas Eckes, "Paternalistic and Envious Gender Stereotypes," 99; Anne M. Koenig, Alice H. Eagly, Abigail A. Mitchell, and Tiina Ristikari, "Are Leader Stereotypes Masculine?," 616.
30. Joan C. Williams and Rachel Dempsey, *What Works for Women at Work*.
31. Ibid.
32. Kerry Ann Rockquemore, "How to Mentor New Faculty."
33. Chesler and Chesler, "Gender-Informed Mentoring Strategies for Women Engineering Scholars," 49; Johnson, *On Being a Mentor*; Kathy E. Kram and Lynn A. Isabella, "Mentoring Alternatives," 110.
34. Monica C. Higgins, Dawn E. Chandler, and Kathy E. Kram, "Developmental Initiation and Developmental Networks," 349; Higgins and David A. Thomas, "Constellations and Careers," 223.

Chapter 9

1. Caryl E. Rusbult, Eli J. Finkel, and Madoka Kumashiro, "The Michelangelo Phenomenon," 305.
2. Belle Rose Ragins, "Relational Mentoring," 519.
3. Rusbult et al., "The Michelangelo Phenomenon," 305.
4. Lucia A. Gilbert and Karen M. Rossman, "Gender and the Mentoring Process for Women," 233; Ragins, "Relational Mentoring," 519.
5. Ellen A. Ensher and Susan E. Murphy, "The Mentoring Relationship Challenges Scale," 253; Hanna Rosin, *The End of Men*.
6. Rosalind C. Barnett and Karen C. Gareis, "Role Theory Perspectives on Work and Family," 209; Mary Blair-Loy, *Competing Devotions*; Brent Mallinckrodt, Frederick T. Leong, and Mary M. Kralj, "Sex Differences in Graduate Student Life-Change Stress and Stress Symptoms," 333; Robin W. Simon, "Parental Role Strains, Salience of Parental Identity and Gender Differences in Psychological Distress," 25.
7. Barnett and Gareis, "Role Theory Perspectives on Work and Family," 209.
8. Etzkowitz et al., *Athena Unbound*.
9. Lois A. Benishek, Kathleen J. Bieschke, Jeeseon Park, and Suzanne M. Slattery, "A Multicultural Feminist Model of Mentoring," 428.
10. Benishek et al., "A Multicultural Feminist Model of Mentoring," 428; Phyllis Moen and Patricia Roehling, *The Career Mystique*; Pamela Stone, *Opting Out?*; Sonya Williams and Shin-Kap Han, "Career Clocks: Forked Roads," 80.

11. Lillian T. Eby, Tammy D. Allen, Sarah C. Evans, Thomas Ng, and David L. DuBois, "Does Mentoring Matter?," 254.

12. Etzkowitz et al., *Athena Unbound*.

13. Joan Jeruchim and Patricia Gottlieb Shapiro, *Women, Mentors, and Success*.

14. Naomi C. Chesler and Mark A. Chesler, "Gender-Informed Mentoring Strategies for Women Engineering Scholars," 49; Margaret M. Hopkins, Deborah A. O'Neil, Angela Passarelli, and Diana Bilimoria, "Women's Leadership Development: Strategic Practices for Women and Organizations," 348; Ragins, "Relational Mentoring," 519.

15. Joan C. Williams and Rachel Dempsey, *What Works for Women at Work*.

16. Rachel Nickless, "Lifelong Confidence Rewarded in Bigger Pay Packets."

17. Monica C. Higgins, Shoshana R. Dobrow, and Dawn Chandler, "Never Quite Good Enough," 207.

18. Albert Bandura, *Self-Efficacy*.

19. Belle Rose Ragins and Kathy E. Kram, *The Handbook of Mentoring at Work*.

20. W. Brad Johnson, *On Being a Mentor*.

21. Janell C. Fetterolf and Alice H. Eagly, "Do Young Women Expect Gender Equality in Their Future Lives?," 83; Hazel Markus and Paula Nurius, "Possible Selves," 954.

22. W. Brad Johnson and Charles R. Ridley, *The Elements of Mentoring*.

23. Samuel J. Marwit and Clayton Lessor, "Role of Deceased Mentors in the Ongoing Lives of Proteges," 125.

24. Terence R. Mitchell and Denise Daniels, "Motivation," 225.

25. Robert Rosenthal and Lenore Jacobson, *Pygmalion in the Classroom*.

26. Elisha Y. Babad, Jacinto Inbar, and Robert Rosenthal, "Pygmalion, Galatea, and the Golem," 459.

27. Williams and Dempsey, *What Works for Women at Work*.

28. Rosin, *The End of Men*.

29. Sheryl Sandberg, *Lean In*.

30. Etzkowitz et al., *Athena Unbound*.

31. Alice H. Eagly and Linda L. Carli, *Through the Labyrinth*.

32. Rosin, *The End of Men*.

33. Peggy Drexler, "Why You Need to Brag More (And How to Do It)"; Madeline E. Heilman and Michelle C. Haynes, "No Credit Where Credit Is Due," 905.

34. Michelle C. Haynes and Madeline E. Heilman, "It Had to Be You (Not Me)!"

35. Barbara B. Stonewater, Sonja A. Eveslage, and Michael R. Dingerson, "Gender Differences in Career Helping Relationships," 72.

36. Chesler and Chesler, "Gender-Informed Mentoring Strategies for Women Engineering Scholars," 49.

37. Williams and Dempsey, *What Works for Women at Work.*

38. Etzkowitz et al., *Athena Unbound.*

39. David G. Smith, *Developing Pathways to Serving Together.*

40. Ragins and Kram, *The Handbook of Mentoring at Work.*

Chapter 10

1. Terri A. Scandura and Ethlyn A. Williams, "An Investigation of the Moderating Effects of Gender on the Relationships Between Mentorship Initiation and Protégé Perceptions of Mentoring Functions," 342.

2. David P. Schmitt, "Are Women More Emotional Than Men?"

3. Alice H. Eagly and Jean Lau Chin, "Diversity and Leadership in a Changing World," 216.

4. Tara Mohr, "Why Women Don't Apply for Jobs Unless They're 100% Qualified."

5. Alice H. Eagly and Linda L. Carli, *Through the Labyrinth*; Scandura and Williams, "An Investigation of the Moderating Effects of Gender on the Relationships Between Mentorship Initiation and Protégé Perceptions of Mentoring Functions," 342.

6. Peter Glick and Susan T. Fiske, "The Ambivalent Sexism Inventory," 491.

7. Glick and Fiske, "The Ambivalent Sexism Inventory," 491; Kristen Jones, Kathy Stewart, Eden King, Whitney Botsford Morgan, Veronica Gilrane, and Kimberly Hylton, "Negative Consequence of Benevolent Sexism on Efficacy and Performance," 171; Melanie Tannenbaum, "The Problem When Sexism Just Sounds So Darn Friendly…"

8. Adam Grant, "Why So Many Men Don't Stand Up for Their Female Colleagues."

9. Robert T. Blackburn, David W. Chapman, and Susan M. Cameron, "'Cloning' in Academe," 315.

10. W. Brad Johnson and Charles R. Ridley, *The Elements of Mentoring*; Sheryl Sandberg, *Lean In.*

11. Scandura and Williams, "An Investigation of the Moderating Effects of Gender on the Relationships Between Mentorship Initiation and Protégé Perceptions of Mentoring Functions," 342.

12. Ibid.

13. W. Brad Johnson, *On Being a Mentor.*

14. Amy E. Hurley, "Challenges in Cross-Gender Mentoring Relationships," 42.

15. Kathy E. Kram, "Improving the Mentoring Process."

16. Robert J. Sternberg, "A Triangular Theory of Love," 119.

17. Joan Jeruchim and Patricia Gottlieb Shapiro, *Women, Mentors, and Success.*

18. Sternberg, "A Triangular Theory of Love," 119.

19. Hurley, "Challenges in Cross-Gender Mentoring Relationships," 42; Johnson, *On Being a Mentor.*

20. S. Michael Plaut, "Boundary Issues in Teacher–Student Relationships," 210; Peter Rutter, *Sex in the Forbidden Zone.*

21. Lawton Wehle Fitt and Derek A. Newton, "When the Mentor Is a Man and the Protege a Woman," 56; Jeruchim and Shapiro, *Women, Mentors, and Success*; Johnson, *On Being a Mentor*; Johnson and Ridley, *The Elements of Mentoring*; Plaut, "Boundary Issues in Teacher-Student Relationships," 210; Rutter, *Sex in the Forbidden Zone.*

22. James G. Clawson and Kathy E. Kram, "Managing Cross-Gender Mentoring," 22; Johnson, *On Being a Mentor*; Belle Rose Ragins and Kathy E. Kram, *The Handbook of Mentoring at Work.*

23. Fitt and Newton, "When the Mentor Is a Man and the Protege a Woman," 56; Kram, "Improving the Mentoring Process"; Lillian B. Rubin, *Just Friends.*

REFERENCES

Allen, Tammy D. "Mentoring Others: A Dispositional and Motivational Approach." *Journal of Vocational Behavior* 62 (2003): 134–54.

Andersen, Steffen, Seda Ertac, Uri Gneezy, John A. List, and Sandra Maximiano. "Gender, Competitiveness, and Socialization at a Young Age: Evidence from a Matrilineal and a Patriarchal Society." *Review of Economics and Statistics* 95 (2013): 1438–43.

Annis, Barbara, and John Gray. *Work with Me: The 8 Blind Spots Between Men and Women in Business*. New York: Macmillan, 2013.

Babad, Elisha Y., Jacinto Inbar, and Robert Rosenthal. "Pygmalion, Galatea, and the Golem: Investigations of Biased and Unbiased Teachers." *Journal of Educational Psychology* 74 (1982): 459–474.

Bandura, Albert. *Self-Efficacy: The Exercise of Self-Control*. New York: W. H. Freeman & Company, 1997.

Barnett, Rosalind C., and Karen C. Gareis. "Role Theory Perspectives on Work and Family." In *The Work and Family Handbook: Multi-Disciplinary Perspectives and Approaches*, edited by Marcie Pitt-Catsouphes, Ellen Ernst Kossek, and Stephen Sweet, 209–21. Mahwah, NJ: Lawrence Erlbaum Associates, 2006.

Baudouin, Jean-Yves, and Guy Tiberghien. "Symmetry, Averageness, and Feature Size in the Facial Attractiveness of Women." *Acta Psychologica* 117 (2004): 313–32.

Benishek, Lois A., Kathleen J. Bieschke, Jeeseon Park, and Suzanne M. Slattery. "A Multicultural Feminist Model of Mentoring." *Journal of Multicultural Counseling and Development* 32 (2004): 428–42.

Berdahl, Jennifer L., and Celia Moore. "Workplace Harassment: Double Jeopardy for Minority Women." *Journal of Applied Psychology* 91 (2006): 426–36.

Beyer, Sylvia. "Gender Differences in the Accuracy of Self-Evaluations of Performance." *Journal of Personality and Social Psychology* 59 (1990): 960–70.

Blackburn, Robert T., David W. Chapman, and Susan M. Cameron. "'Cloning' in Academe: Mentorship and Academic Careers." *Research in Higher Education* 15 (1981): 315–27.

Blair-Loy, Mary. *Competing Devotions: Career and Family Among Women Executives.* Boston: Harvard University Press, 2009.

Bleske-Rechek, April, Erin Somers, Cierra Micke, Leah Erickson, Lindsay Matteson, Corey Stocco, Brittany Schumacher, and Laura Ritchie. "Benefit or Burden? Attraction in Cross-Sex Friendship." *Journal of Social and Personal Relationships* 29 (2012): 569–96.

Booth, Alison, and Patrick Nolen. "Choosing to Compete: How Different Are Girls and Boys?" *Journal of Economic Behavior & Organization* 81 (2012): 542–55.

Bowen, Chieh-Chen, Janet K. Swim, and Rick R. Jacobs. "Evaluating Gender Biases on Actual Job Performance of Real People: A Meta-Analysis." *Journal of Applied Social Psychology* 30 (2000): 2194–215.

Budig, Michelle J., and Paula England. "The Wage Penalty for Motherhood." *American Sociological Review* 66 (2001): 204–25.

Burke, Ronald J., and Carol A. McKeen. "Gender Effects in Mentoring Relationships." *Journal of Social Behavior and Personality* 11 (1996): 91–104.

Burke, Ronald J., and Eddy Ng. "The Changing Nature of Work and Organizations: Implications for Human Resource Management." *Human Resource Management Review* 16 (2006): 86–94.

Buser, Thomas, and Noemi Peter. "Multitasking." *Experimental Economics* 15 (2012): 641–55.

Buss, David M. "The Great Struggles of Life: Darwin and the Emergence of Evolutionary Psychology." *American Psychologist* 64 (2009): 140–48.

Canli, Turhan, John E. Desmond, Zuo Zhao, and John D. Gabrieli. "Sex Differences in the Neural Basis of Emotional Memories." *Proceedings of the National Academy of Sciences* 99 (2002): 10,789–94.

Charyton, Christine, John O. Elliott, Mohammed A. Rahman, Jeness L. Woodard, and Samantha DeDios. "Gender and Science: Women Nobel Laureates." *The Journal of Creative Behavior* 45 (2011): 203–14.

Chesler, Naomi C., and Mark A. Chesler. "Gender-Informed Mentoring Strategies for Women Engineering Scholars: On Establishing a Caring Community." *Journal of Engineering Education* 91 (2002): 49–55.

Clawson, James G., and Kathy E. Kram. "Managing Cross-Gender Mentoring." *Business Horizons* 27 (1984): 22–32.

Correll, Shelley J., and Stephen Benard. "Getting a Job: Is There a Motherhood Penalty?" *American Journal of Sociology* 112 (2007): 1297–1339.

Committee on Maximizing the Potential of Women in Academic Science and Engineering, National Academy of Sciences, National Academy of Engineering, and Institute of Medicine. *Biological, Social, and Organizational Components of Success for Women in Academic Science and Engineering: Workshop Report.* Washington, DC: National Academies Press, 2006.

Croson, Rachel, and Uri Gneezy. "Gender Differences in Preferences." *Journal of Economic Literature* 47 (2009): 448–74.

Davies, Paul G., Steven J. Spencer, and Claude M. Steele. "Clearing the Air: Identity Safety Moderates the Effects of Stereotype Threat on Women's Leadership Aspirations." *Journal of Personality and Social Psychology* 88 (2005): 276–87.

Davis, Lori L., Marc S. Little, and William L. Thornton. "The Art and Angst of the Mentoring Relationship." *Academic Psychiatry* 21 (1997): 61–71.

DeSante, Christopher D. "Working Twice As Hard to Get Half As Far: Race, Work Ethic, and America's Deserving Poor." *American Journal of Political Science* 57 (2013): 342–56.

Dickinson, Katy, Tanya Jankot, and Helen Gracon. "Sun Mentoring: 1996–2009." Technical Report, Sun Labs, Menlo Park, CA, 2009.

Dreher, George F., and Ronald A. Ash. "A Comparative Study of Mentoring Among Men and Women in Managerial, Professional, and Technical Positions." *Journal of Applied Psychology* 75 (1990): 539–46.

Drexler, Peggy. "Why You Need to Brag More (And How to Do It)." *Forbes*, August 23, 2013. Accessed February 23, 2016. http://www.forbes.com/sites/peggydrexler/2013/08/23/why-you-need-to-brag-more-and-how-to-do-it/#2715e4857a0b348b754b3929.

Drexler, Peggy. "Women on Capitol Hill Barred from Time Alone with Male Bosses?" CNN, May 18, 2015. Accessed February 23, 2016. http://edition.cnn.com/2015/05/18/opinions/drexler-women-on-capitol-hill/.

Dweck, Carol. *Mindset: The New Psychology of Success.* New York: Random House, 2006.

Eagly, Alice H., and Linda L. Carli. *Through the Labyrinth: The Truth About How Women Become Leaders*. Boston: Harvard Business Press, 2007.

Eagly, Alice H., and Jean Lau Chin. "Diversity and Leadership in a Changing World." *American Psychologist* 65 (2010): 216–24.

Eagly, Alice H., and Blair T. Johnson. "Gender and Leadership Style: A Meta-Analysis." *Psychological Bulletin* 108 (1990): 233–56.

Eagly, Alice H., and Steven J. Karau. "Role Congruity Theory of Prejudice Toward Female Leaders." *Psychological Review* 109 (2002): 573–98.

Eby, Lillian T., Tammy D. Allen, Sarah C. Evans, Thomas Ng, and David L. DuBois. "Does Mentoring Matter? A Multidisciplinary Meta-Analysis Comparing Mentored and Non-Mentored Individuals." *Journal of Vocational Behavior* 72 (2008): 254–67.

Eckes, Thomas. "Paternalistic and Envious Gender Stereotypes: Testing Predictions from the Stereotype Content Model." *Sex Roles* 47 (2002): 99–114.

Effron, Daniel A., and Dale T. Miller. "How the Moralization of Issues Grants Social Legitimacy to Act on One's Attitudes." *Personality and Social Psychology Bulletin* 38 (2012): 690–701.

Elliott, Catherine, Joanne D. Leck, Barbara Orser, and Catherine Mossop. "An Exploration of Gender and Trust in Mentoring Relationships." *Journal of Diversity Management* 1 (2011): 1–12.

Elsesser, Kim. *Sex and the Office: Women, Men, and the Sex Partition That's Dividing the Workplace*. Lanham, MD: Rowman & Littlefield, 2015.

Ensher, Ellen A., and Susan E. Murphy. "The Mentoring Relationship Challenges Scale: The Impact of Mentoring Stage, Type, and Gender." *Journal of Vocational Behavior* 79 (2011): 253–66.

Etzkowitz, Henry, Carol Kemelgor, and Brian Uzzi. *Athena Unbound: The Advancement of Women in Science and Technology*. Boston: Cambridge University Press, 2000.

Fagenson, Ellen A. "The Power of a Mentor: Protégés' and Nonprotégés' Perceptions of Their Own Power in Organizations." *Group & Organization Management* 13 (1988): 182–94.

Feist-Price, Sonja. "Cross-Gender Mentoring Relationships: Critical Issues." *Journal of Rehabilitation* 60 (1994): 13–17.

Fels, Anna. "Do Women Lack Ambition?" *Harvard Business Review* 82 (2004): 50–60.

Fetterolf, Janell C., and Alice H. Eagly. "Do Young Women Expect Gender Equality in Their Future Lives? An Answer from a Possible Selves Experiment." *Sex Roles* 65 (2011): 83–93.

Fitt, Lawton Wehle, and Derek A. Newton. "When the Mentor Is a Man and the Protege a Woman." *Harvard Business Review* 59 (1981): 56–60.

Fullerton, Howard N. "Labor Force Participation: 75 Years of Change, 1950–98 and 1998–2025." *Monthly Labor Review* 122 (1999): 3–12.

Gervais, Sarah J., Theresa K. Vescio, Jens Förster, Anne Maass, and Caterina Suitner. "Seeing Women As Objects: The Sexual Body Part Recognition Bias." *European Journal of Social Psychology* 42 (2012): 743–53.

Gerzema, John, and Michael D'Antonio. *The Athena Doctrine: How Women (and the Men Who Think Like Them) Will Rule the Future.* San Francisco: John Wiley & Sons, 2013.

Gilbert, Lucia A. "Female and Male Emotional Dependency and Its Implications for the Therapist-Client Relationship." *Professional Psychology: Research and Practice* 18 (1987): 555–61.

Gilbert, Lucia A., and Karen M. Rossman. "Gender and the Mentoring Process for Women: Implications for Professional Development." *Professional Psychology: Research and Practice* 23 (1992): 233–38.

Glick, Peter, and Susan T. Fiske. "The Ambivalent Sexism Inventory: Differentiating Hostile and Benevolent Sexism." *Journal of Personality and Social Psychology* 70 (1996): 491–512.

Goldin, Claudia, and Cecilia Rouse. "Orchestrating Impartiality: The Impact of 'Blind' Auditions on Female Musicians." *American Economic Review* 90 (2000): 715–41.

Grammer, Karl, Bernhard Fink, and Nick Neave. "Human Pheromones and Sexual Attraction." *European Journal of Obstetrics & Gynecology and Reproductive Biology* 118 (2005): 135–42.

Grammer, Karl, and Randy Thornhill. "Human (Homo sapiens) Facial Attractiveness and Sexual Selection: The Role of Symmetry and Averageness." *Journal of Comparative Psychology* 108 (1994): 233–42.

Grant, Adam. "Why So Many Men Don't Stand Up for Their Female Colleagues," *Atlantic*, April 29, 2014. Accessed February 23, 2016. http://www.theatlantic.com/business/archive/2014/04/why-men-dont-stand-up-for-women-to-lead/361231/.

Greenberg, Alissa. "A Nobel Scientist Just Made a Breathtakingly Sexist Speech at International Conference," *Time*, June 10, 2015. Accessed April 14, 2016. http://time.com/3915617/women-science-tim-hunt-nobel-sexist/.

Haggard, Dana L., and Daniel B. Turban. "The Mentoring Relationship As a Context for Psychological Contract Development." *Journal of Applied Social Psychology* 42 (2012): 1904–31.

Halpern, Diane F. *Sex Differences in Cognitive Abilities.* New York: Psychology Press, 2013.

Hansman, Catherine A. "Mentoring and Women's Career Development." *New Directions for Adult and Continuing Education* 80 (1998): 63–71.

Harden, Sherry L., Richard A. Clark, W. Brad Johnson, and Joshua Larson. "Cross-Gender Mentorship in Clinical Psychology Doctoral Programs: An Exploratory Survey Study." *Mentoring & Tutoring: Partnership in Learning* 17 (2009): 277–90.

Harvard Health Publications. "Mars vs. Venus: The Gender Gap in Health," *Harvard Men's Health Watch,* January 1, 2010. Accessed February 23, 2016. http://www.health.harvard.edu/newsletter_article/mars-vs-venus-the-gender-gap-in-health.

Haynes, Michelle C., and Madeline E. Heilman. "It Had to Be You (Not Me)! Women's Attributional Rationalization of Their Contribution to Successful Joint Work Outcomes." *Personality and Social Psychology Bulletin* (2013). Accessed February 23, 2016. doi: 10.1177/0146167213486358.

Headley, Jason. "It's Not About the Nail," YouTube video, 1:41, May 22, 2013, https://www.youtube.com/watch?v=-4EDhdAHrOg.

Heilman, Madeline E., and Michelle C. Haynes. "No Credit Where Credit Is Due: Attributional Rationalization of Women's Success in Male-Female Teams." *Journal of Applied Psychology* 90 (2005): 905–16.

Hewlett, Sylvia Ann, Kerrie Peraino, Laura Sherbin, and Karen Sumberg. *The Sponsor Effect: Breaking Through the Last Glass Ceiling.* Cambridge: Harvard Business Review, 2010.

Higgins, Monica C., Dawn E. Chandler, and Kathy E. Kram. "Developmental Initiation and Developmental Networks." In *The Handbook of Mentoring at Work: Theory, Research, and Practice*, edited by Belle Rose Ragins and Kathy Kram, 349–72. Thousand Oaks, CA: Sage Publications, 2007.

Higgins, Monica C., Shoshana R. Dobrow, and Dawn Chandler. "Never Quite Good Enough: The Paradox of Sticky Developmental Relationships for Elite University Graduates." *Journal of Vocational Behavior* 72 (2008): 207–24.

Higgins, Monica C., and David A. Thomas. "Constellations and Careers: Toward Understanding the Effects of Multiple Developmental Relationships." *Journal of Organizational Behavior* 22 (2001): 223–47.

Hook, Joshua N., Don E. Davis, Jesse Owen, Everett L. Worthington Jr., and Shawn O. Utsey. "Cultural Humility: Measuring Openness to Culturally Diverse Clients." *Journal of Counseling Psychology* 60 (2013): 353–66.

Hopkins, Margaret M., Deborah A. O'Neil, Angela Passarelli, and Diana Bilimoria. "Women's Leadership Development: Strategic Practices for Women and Organizations." *Consulting Psychology Journal: Practice and Research* 60 (2008): 348–65.

Hoyt, Crystal L., and Jim Blascovich. "Leadership Efficacy and Women Leaders' Responses to Stereotype Activation." *Group Processes & Intergroup Relations* 10 (2007): 595–616.

Hurley, Amy E. "Challenges in Cross-Gender Mentoring Relationships: Psychological Intimacy, Myths, Rumours, Innuendoes and Sexual Harassment." *Leadership & Organization Development Journal* 17 (1996): 42–49.

Ibarra, Herminia, Nancy M. Carter, and Christine Silva. "Why Men Still Get More Promotions Than Women." *Harvard Business Review* 88 (2010): 80–85.

Inesi, M. Ena, and Daniel M. Cable. "When Accomplishments Come Back to Haunt You: The Negative Effect of Competence Signals on Women's Performance Evaluations." *Personnel Psychology* 68 (2015): 615–57.

Jeanquart-Barone, Sandy, and Uma Sekaran. "Effects of Supervisor's Gender on American Women's Trust." *The Journal of Social Psychology* 134 (1994): 253–55.

Jeruchim, Joan, and Patricia Gottlieb Shapiro. *Women, Mentors, and Success.* New York: Fawcett Columbine, 1992.

Joel, Daphna, Zohar Berman, Ido Tavor, Nadav Wexler, Olga Gaber, Yaniv Stein, Nisan Shefi et al. "Sex Beyond the Genitalia: The Human Brain Mosaic." *Proceedings of the National Academy of Sciences* 112 (2015): 15,468–73.

Johns, Michael, Toni Schmader, and Andy Martens. "Knowing Is Half the Battle: Teaching Stereotype Threat As a Means of Improving Women's Math Performance." *Psychological Science* 16 (2005): 175–179.

Johnson, W. Brad. *On Being a Mentor: A Guide for Higher Education Faculty.* 2nd Ed. New York: Routledge, 2015.

Johnson, W. Brad, and Charles R. Ridley. *The Elements of Mentoring.* Rev. ed. New York: Palgrave Macmillan, 2008.

Jones, Kristen, Kathy Stewart, Eden King, Whitney Botsford Morgan, Veronica Gilrane, and Kimberly Hylton. "Negative Consequence of Benevolent Sexism on Efficacy and Performance." *Gender in Management: An International Journal* 29 (2014): 171–89.

Kabat-Farr, Dana, and Lilia M. Cortina. "Selective Incivility: Gender, Race, and the Discriminatory Workplace." *Gender and the Dysfunctional Workplace* (2012): 120–34.

Kalbfleisch, Pamela J. "Appeasing the Mentor." *Aggressive Behavior* 23 (1997): 389–403.

Kalbfleisch, Pamela J., and Joann Keyton. "Power and Equality in Mentoring Relationships." *Gender, Power, and Communication in Human Relationships* (1995): 189–212.

Kanter, Rosabeth Moss. *Men and Women of the Corporation*. New York: Basic Books, 1993.

Keith, Kent M. *Anyway: The Paradoxical Commandments: Finding Personal Meaning in a Crazy World*. New York: Penguin, 2004.

Koenig, Anne M., Alice H. Eagly, Abigail A. Mitchell, and Tiina Ristikari. "Are Leader Stereotypes Masculine? A Meta-Analysis of Three Research Paradigms." *Psychological Bulletin* 137 (2011): 616–42.

Kram, Kathy E. "Improving the Mentoring Process." *Training & Development Journal* (1985).

Kram, Kathy E., and Lynn A. Isabella. "Mentoring Alternatives: The Role of Peer Relationships in Career Development." *Academy of Management Journal* 28 (1985): 110–32.

Kray, Laura J., and Michael P. Haselhuhn. "Male Pragmatism in Negotiators' Ethical Reasoning." *Journal of Experimental Social Psychology* 48 (2012): 1124–31.

Lawson, Raef A. "Is Classroom Cheating Related to Business Students' Propensity to Cheat in the 'Real World'?" *Journal of Business Ethics* 49 (2004): 189–99.

Lee, Lind-Eling, Ric Marshall, Damion Rallis, and Matt Moscardi. "Women on Boards: Global Trends in Gender Diversity on Corporate Boards," MSCI, November 2015. Accessed February 23, 2016. https://www.msci.com/documents/10199/04b6f646 -d638-4878-9c61-4eb91748a82b.

Liang, Belle, Allison J. Tracy, Catherine A. Taylor, and Linda M. Williams. "Mentoring College-Age Women: A Relational Approach." *American Journal of Community Psychology* 30 (2002): 271–88.

Lutter, Mark. "Do Women Suffer from Network Closure? The Moderating Effect of Social Capital on Gender Inequality in a Project-Based Labor Market, 1929 to 2010." *American Sociological Review* (2015). Accessed February 22, 2016. doi:10.177/0003122414568788.

Makhanova, Anastasia, and Saul L. Miller. "Female Fertility and Male Mating: Women's Ovulatory Cues Influence Men's Physiology, Cognition, and Behavior." *Social and Personality Psychology Compass* 7 (2013): 389–400.

Mallinckrodt, Brent, Frederick T. Leong, and Mary M. Kralj. "Sex Differences in Graduate Student Life-Change Stress and Stress Symptoms." *Journal of College Student Development* 30 (1989): 333–38.

Maner, Jon K., and James K. McNulty. "Attunement to the Fertility Status of Same-Sex Rivals: Women's Testosterone Responses to Olfactory Ovulation Cues." *Evolution and Human Behavior* 34 (2013): 412–18.

Markus, Hazel, and Paula Nurius. "Possible Selves." *American Psychologist* 41 (1986): 954–69.

Marwit, Samuel J., and Clayton Lessor. "Role of Deceased Mentors in the Ongoing Lives of Proteges." *Journal of Death and Dying* 41 (2000): 125–38.

McKeen, Carol A., and Ronald J. Burke. "Mentor Relationships in Organisations: Issues, Strategies and Prospects for Women." *Journal of Management Development* 8 (1989): 33–42.

McKinsey & Company. *Women in the Workplace.* Accessed November 29, 2015. http://womenintheworkplace.com/.

McLearn, Kathryn Taaffe, Diane Colasanto, and Cathy Schoen. *Mentoring Makes a Difference: Findings from the Commonwealth Fund: 1998 Survey of Adults Mentoring Young People.* Commonwealth Fund, 1998.

McRae, Kateri, Kevin N. Ochsner, Iris B. Mauss, John J. Gabrieli, and James J. Gross. "Gender Differences in Emotion Regulation: An fMRI Study of Cognitive Reappraisal." *Group Processes & Intergroup Relations* 11 (2008): 143–62.

Meyerson, Debra. *Tempered Radicals.* Boston: Harvard Business School, 2001.

Milkman, Katherine L., Modupe Akinola, and Dolly Chugh. "What Happens Before? A Field Experiment Exploring How Pay and Representation Differentially Shape Bias on the Pathway into Organizations." *Journal of Applied Psychology* 100 (2015): 1678–712.

Mimms, Sarah. "Why Some Male Members of Congress Won't Be Alone with Female Staffers," *National Journal,* May 14, 2015. Accessed February 23, 2016. https://www.nationaljournal.com/s/27043/why-some-male-members-congress-wont-be-alone-with-female-staffers?ref=facebook.com&mrefid=dcwomen1.

Mitchell, Terence R., and Denise Daniels. "Motivation." In *Handbook of Psychology,* edited by Walter C. Borman, Daniel R. Ilgen, Richard J. Klimoski, vol. 12, 225–254. Hoboken, NJ: John Wiley & Sons, 2003.

Moen, Phyllis, and Patricia Roehling. *The Career Mystique: Cracks in the American Dream.* Lanham, MD: Rowman & Littlefield, 2005.

Mohr, Tara. "Why Women Don't Apply for Jobs Unless They're 100% Qualified." *Harvard Business Review* (2014).

Mullen, Carol A. *Mentorship Primer.* New York: Peter Lang, 2005.

Myers, Scott A., Gregory A. Cranmer, Zachary W. Goldman, Michael Sollitto, Hailey G. Gillen, and Hannah Ball. "Differences in Information Seeking Among Organizational Peers: Perceptions of Appropriateness, Importance, and Frequency." *International Journal of Business Communication* (2015). Accessed February 23, 2016. doi: 10.1177/2329488415573928.

Nickless, Rachel. "Lifelong Confidence Rewarded in Bigger Pay Packets." *Australian Financial Review*. November 28, 2012. Accessed February 23, 2016. http://origin-www.afr.com/p/national/work_space/lifelong_confidence _rewarded_in_gSNmV78QAuqjmT8Ksy3QSJ.

Nierenberg, S., and C. Marvin. "Women 'Take Care,' Men 'Take Charge': Stereotyping of US Business Leaders Exposed." New York: Catalyst (2006).

Noe, Raymond A. "An Investigation of the Determinants of Successful Assigned Mentoring Relationships." *Personnel Psychology* 41 (1988): 457–79.

Offer, Shira, and Barbara Schneider. "Revisiting the Gender Gap in Time-Use Patterns: Multitasking and Well-Being Among Mothers and Fathers in Dual-Earner Families." *American Sociological Review* 76 (2011): 809–33.

Parker, Kim. *5 Facts About Today's Fathers*. Pew Research Center. Accessed February 22, 2016. http://www.pewresearch.org/fact-tank/2015/06/18/5-facts-about-todays -fathers/.

Plaut, S. Michael. "Boundary Issues in Teacher-Student Relationships." *Journal of Sex & Marital Therapy* 19 (1993): 210–19.

Pleck, Joseph H. *The Myth of Masculinity*. Boston: MIT Press, 1981.

Prime, Jeanine, Mike Otterman, and Elizabeth R. Salib. "Engaging Men Through Inclusive Leadership." In *Gender in Organizations: Are Men Allies or Adversaries to Women's Career Advancement?*, edited by Ronald J. Burke and Debra A. Major, 385–404. Cheltenham, MA: Edward Elgar, 2014.

Ragins, Belle Rose. "Relational Mentoring: A Positive Approach to Mentoring at Work." In *The Oxford Handbook of Positive Organizational Scholarship*, edited by Kim S. Cameron and Gretchen M. Spreitzer, 519–536. Oxford, UK: Oxford University Press, 2011.

Ragins, Belle Rose, and John L. Cotton. "Mentor Functions and Outcomes: A Comparison of Men and Women in Formal and Informal Mentoring Relationships." *Journal of Applied Psychology* 84 (1999): 529–50.

Ragins, Belle Rose, and Kathy E. Kram. *The Handbook of Mentoring at Work: Theory, Research, and Practice*. Thousand Oaks, CA: Sage Publications, 2007.

Ragins, Belle Rose, and Dean B. McFarlin. "Perceptions of Mentor Roles in Cross-Gender Mentoring Relationships." *Journal of Vocational Behavior* 37 (1990): 321–39.

Ratner, Rebecca K., and Dale T. Miller. "The Norm of Self-Interest and Its Effects on Social Action." *Journal of Personality and Social Psychology* 81 (2001): 5–16.

Rockquemore, Kerry Ann. "How to Mentor New Faculty: A New Model of Mentoring." *Inside Higher Ed*, July 22, 2013. https://www.insidehighered.com/advice/2013/07/22/essay-calling-senior-faculty-embrace-new-style-mentoring.

Rogers, Carl R. "The Necessary and Sufficient Conditions of Therapeutic Personality Change." *Journal of Consulting Psychology* 21 (1957): 95–103.

Rosenthal, Robert, and Lenore Jacobson. *Pygmalion in the Classroom: Teacher Expectation and Pupils' Intellectual Development*. New York: Holt, Rinehart & Winston, 1968.

Rosin, Hanna. *The End of Men: And the Rise of Women*. New York: Penguin, 2012.

Rubin, Lillian B. *Just Friends: The Role of Friendship in Our Lives*. New York: Harper Perennial, 1986.

Rusbult, Caryl E., Eli J. Finkel, and Madoka Kumashiro. "The Michelangelo Phenomenon." *Current Directions in Psychological Science* 18 (2009): 305–09.

Rutter, Peter. *Sex in the Forbidden Zone: When Men in Power—Therapists, Doctors, Clergy, Teachers, and Others—Betray Women's Trust*. Los Angeles: Jeremy P. Tarcher, Inc., 1989.

Sandberg, Sheryl. *Lean In: Women, Work, and the Will to Lead*. New York: Random House, 2013.

Sanford, Amy Aldridge, Elaina M. Ross, Shawna J. Blake, and Renée L. Cambiano. "Finding Courage and Confirmation: Resisting Impostor Feelings Through Relationships with Mentors, Romantic Partners, and Other Women in Leadership." *Advancing Women in Leadership* 35 (2015): 31–41.

Scandura, Terri A., and Ethlyn A. Williams. "An Investigation of the Moderating Effects of Gender on the Relationships Between Mentorship Initiation and Protégé Perceptions of Mentoring Functions." *Journal of Vocational Behavior* 59 (2001): 342–63.

Schmitt, David P. "Are Women More Emotional Than Men?" *Psychology Today*, April 10, 2015. Accessed February 23, 2016. https://www.psychologytoday.com/blog/sexual-personalities/201504/are-women-more-emotional-men.

Seck, Hope H. "Controversy Surrounds Firing of Marines' Female Recruit Battalion CO," *Marine Corps Times*, July 15, 2015. Accessed April 14, 2016. http://www.marinecorpstimes.com/story/military/2015/07/07/kate-germano-fired-marine-corps-female-recruit-unit-commander/29763371/.

Sharpnack, Rayona. "What Do Men Get Out of Advancing Women?" *Diversity Best Practices.* July 27, 2015. http://www.diversitybestpractices.com.

Simon, Robin W. "Parental Role Strains, Salience of Parental Identity and Gender Differences in Psychological Distress." *Journal of Health and Social Behavior* (1992): 25–35.

Singh, Devendra, Barbara J. Dixson, Thomas S. Jessop, Bethan Morgan, and Alan F. Dixson. "Cross-Cultural Consensus for Waist–Hip Ratio and Women's Attractiveness." *Evolution and Human Behavior* 31 (2010): 176–81.

Smith, David G. "Developing Pathways to Serving Together: Military Family Life Course and Decision-Making of Dual Military Couples." PhD diss., University of Maryland, 2010.

Spencer, Steven J., Claude M. Steele, and Diane M. Quinn. "Stereotype Threat and Women's Math Performance." *Journal of Experimental Social Psychology* 35 (1999): 4–28.

Sternberg, Robert J. "A Triangular Theory of Love." *Psychological Review* 93 (1986): 119–35.

Stone, Pamela. *Opting Out?: Why Women Really Quit Careers and Head Home.* Berkeley, CA: University of California Press, 2007.

Stonewater, Barbara B., Sonja A. Eveslage, and Michael R. Dingerson. "Gender Differences in Career Helping Relationships." *The Career Development Quarterly* 39 (1990): 72–85.

Tannenbaum, Melanie. "The Problem When Sexism Just Sounds So Darn Friendly...," *Scientific American*, April 2, 2013. Accessed February 23, 2016. http://blogs.scientificamerican.com/psysociety/benevolent-sexism/.

Taylor, Shelley E. *The Tending Instinct: How Nurturing Is Essential to Who We Are and How We Live.* New York: Macmillan, 2002.

Terjesen, Siri, Ruth Sealy, and Val Singh. "Women Directors on Corporate Boards: A Review and Research Agenda." *Corporate Governance: An International Review* 17 (2009): 320–37.

U.S. Bureau of Labor Statistics. *Women in the Labor Force: A Databook.* BLS Report 1052, December 2014. http://www.bls.gov/opub/reports/cps/women-in-the-labor-force-a-databook-2015.pdf.

U.S. Department of Defense. *Implementation of the Full Integration of Women in the Armed Forces.* Accessed December 6, 2015. http://www.defense.gov/Portals/1/Documents/pubs/OSD014303-15.pdf.

U.S. Department of the Navy. *Department of the Navy Talent Management Initiatives.* Accessed November 29, 2015. http://www.secnav.navy.mil/innovation/Documents/2015/05/TalentManagementInitiatives.pdf.

van Hemert, Dianne A., Fons J. van de Vijver, and Ad J. Vingerhoets. "Culture and Crying Prevalences and Gender Differences." *Cross-Cultural Research* 45 (2011): 399–431.

Vigil, Jacob Miguel. "A Socio-Relational Framework of Sex Differences in the Expression of Emotion." *Behavioral and Brain Sciences* 32 (2009): 375–390.

Wang, Wendy, Kim C. Parker, and Paul Taylor. *Breadwinner Moms: Mothers Are the Sole or Primary Provider in Four-in-Ten Households with Children—Public Conflicted About the Growing Trend.* Pew Research Center, 2013.

West, Candace, and Don H. Zimmerman. "Doing Gender." *Gender & Society* 18 (1987): 125–151.

Whittle, Sarah, Murat Yücel, Marie B. Yap, and Nicholas B. Allen. "Sex Differences in the Neural Correlates of Emotion: Evidence from Neuroimaging." *Biological Psychology* 87 (2011): 319–333.

Williams, Joan C., and Rachel Dempsey. *What Works for Women at Work: Four Patterns Working Women Need to Know.* New York: NYU Press, 2014.

Williams, Sonya, and Shin-Kap Han. "Career Clocks: Forked Roads," In *It's About Time: Couples and Careers,* edited by Phyllis Moen, 80–97. Ithaca, NY: Cornell University Press, 2003.

Wood, Wendy, and Alice H. Eagly. "A Cross-Cultural Analysis of the Behavior of Women and Men: Implications for the Origins of Sex Differences." *Psychological Bulletin* 128 (2002): 699–727.

Zuckerman, Harriet. *Scientific Elite: Nobel Laureates in the United States.* New Brunswick, NJ: Transaction Publishers, 1977.

INDEX

of the same actions by women vs.
men, 7–8
of talented women, 23–24
of women as completely different,
25–26, 67–68
perfectionism, 135–137
performance evaluations, 17
persistence, 11
personal growth, 127–143
assertiveness and, 137–139
career vision and, 127–129
confidence building and, 133–135
excellence vs. perfectionism and,
135–137
professional identity and sense of self
as woman, 141–143
taking credit for accomplishments
and, 139–141
work–life balance and, 129–133
*Personality and Social Psychology
Bulletin,* 140
Petro, Janet, 58, 62, 63
about assumptions and decision
making, 77–78
on exclusivity, 91
on friendship, 82
on political teaching, 103
on power sharing, 113
on promotion by mentors, 112
pheromones, 34
policies, 133
politics, 56, 102–105
possible self, 134–135
power
access to, 9–10
differential between mentor and
mentee, 55
dominance and, 145–147
man scripts and, 61
proactive promotion and, 111–113
sharing, 88–89, 113–115
women as mentors and, 22
power-down relationships, 146
power-with relationships, 88–89
proactivity, 53, 71–73, 75, 111–113

problem solving, 76
professional growth, 99–125
challenges for, 105–108
finding/correcting disparities
and, 121–123
inclusion and, 99–102
insider perspective and, 102–105
leadership style development and,
118–120
network development and, 123–125
proactive promotion and, 111–113
protection and empowerment
in, 108–111
public praise, private correction
and, 115–118
sharing power and, 113–115
prolactin, 34
promotions, 10
career-ambition gap and, 10–12
finding/correcting discrepancies
in, 121–123
mentoring and rate of, 43
of mentors, 53
premature, 151–152
reticence about, 149–151
socialization on competition
and, 14–15
protective man scripts, 7, 38, 39
empowerment and, 108–111
guru mentorship and, 123–125
psychology of relationships, 36–40
psychosocial functions, 127–143
purpose, sense of, 47
Pygmalion effect, 135–137

R
racial bias, 19, 66
Ragins, Belle Rose, 80, 103
reason, emotion and, 147–149
reciprocity, 75, 79–80, 114
recognition, 11–12. *See also*
promotions
ensuring, 20
taking/not taking credit and, 9
reflective power, 113–115

202

Index

ABOUT THE AUTHORS

W. Brad Johnson, PhD, is professor of psychology in the Department of Leadership, Ethics, and Law at the United States Naval Academy, and a faculty associate in the Graduate School of Education at Johns Hopkins University. A clinical psychologist and former Lieutenant Commander in the Navy's Medical Service Corps, Dr. Johnson served as a psychologist at Bethesda Naval Hospital and the Medical Clinic at Pearl Harbor where he was the division head for psychology. He is a fellow of the American Psychological Association and recipient of the Johns Hopkins University Teaching Excellence Award. He has served as chair of the American Psychological Association's Ethics Committee and as president of the Society for Military Psychology. Dr. Johnson is the author of more than one hundred journal articles and book chapters—many on the topic of mentoring—and twelve books, in the areas of mentoring, professional ethics, and counseling. Books of related interest include: *On Being a Mentor: A Guide for Higher Education Faculty* (2nd Ed.) (2015), *The Elements of Mentoring* (Revised Ed.) (2008, with Charles Ridley), *The Elements of Ethics for Professionals* (2008, with Charles Ridley), and *Becoming a Leader the Annapolis Way* (2006, with Greg Harper).

David Smith, PhD, is an active duty U.S. Navy Captain and permanent military professor in the Department of Leadership, Ethics, and Law at the United States Naval Academy, having served four years as the chair. A former Navy pilot, Dr. Smith led diverse organizations of women and men culminating in command of a squadron in combat and flew more than three thousand hours over nineteen years, including combat missions in Iraq and Afghanistan. As a sociologist trained in military sociology and social psychology, he focuses his research in gender, work, and family issues including dual career families, military families, women in the military, and retention of women. Dr. Smith is the author of numerous journal articles and book chapters—many on the topic of gender and the workplace. His most recent publications include: "On the Fast Track: Dual Military Couples Navigating Institutional Structures" in *Contemporary Perspectives in Family Research* (2013), "Dual Military Families: Confronting a Stubborn Military Institution" in *Military Families and War in the 21st Century, Comparative Perspectives* (2015), "Leadership and Peer Behaviors: Women in Combat" in *Military Medicine* (2016) and "Gender and the Military Profession: Early Career Influences, Attitudes and Intentions." in *Armed Forces & Society*.